Deception in the Body of Christ

Deception in the Body of Christ

Unveiled Mysteries and Neurolinguistic Dialectics

Dr. Robert E. Hill

RESOURCE *Publications* • Eugene, Oregon

DECEPTION IN THE BODY OF CHRIST
Unveiled Mysteries and Neurolinguistic Dialectics

Copyright © 2010 Dr. Robert E. Hill. All rights reserved. Except for brief quotations in critical publications or reviews, no part of this book may be reproduced in any manner without prior written permission from the publisher. Write: Permissions, Wipf and Stock Publishers, 199 W. 8th Ave., Suite 3, Eugene, OR 97401.

Resource Publications
An Imprint of Wipf and Stock Publishers
199 W. 8th Ave., Suite 3
Eugene, OR 97401
www.wipfandstock.com

ISBN 13: 978-1-60899-102-0

Manufactured in the U.S.A.

All scripture quotations, unless otherwise indicated, are taken from the Holy Bible, New International Version®, NIV®. Copyright ©1973, 1978, 1984 by Biblica, Inc.™ Used by permission of Zondervan. All rights reserved worldwide.

Contents

Foreword vii
Dedication ix
Preface xi
Acknowledgments xv
Introduction xvii

1 The Mystery of Our Perfect God the Creator and the Paradox of a Perfect Creation Who Committed Sin 1

2 Deception and Its Evolution in the Body of Christ 11

3 God's Intentions and Admonitions Regarding Deception in the Body 18

4 The Beginning Church from Pentecost 22

5 Deception and Dialectics 47

6 The Veil of Moses and the Lack of Knowledge of God 67

Conclusion 79
Endnotes 85
Bibliography 99

Foreword

YOU WILL find Elder Robert E. Hill's first book a fascinating read. Began during his candidacy for elder, the book reflects his insistent questioning of himself about his temperament and readiness to be an elder in the Church of Jesus Christ. Elders, according to Scripture, are entrusted with two basic responsibilities: to govern (Acts 20:28) and to teach (1 Timothy 3:1—7; 5:17). Elder Robert has embraced the notion that to govern is to teach and the aim of teaching is four dimensional: to develop the talents and potentialities of learners; to develop the whole personality and education of the learner in the deepest sense; to correct, edify and guide, protect and impart knowledge and provide nourishment for growth; and, to summon the learner to submit to the authority of the divine message of Scripture. Even the organization of the book serves to document the progressive intensification of his self-probing:

- Do I really understand the major doctrines of Christianity? Can I teach the doctrines of God to an agnostic; can I teach them to be seekers; can I be four dimensional in my teaching?

- If Jesus came back today, am I ready? Does my Christian walk withstand the scrutiny of Christian "salt and light?"

And then Elder Robert, as he is often addressed by congregants of Living Word Church and Fellowship, arrives at questions perhaps too often glossed over:

- The centuries since man fell and was removed from the Garden of Eden have made the deleterious consequences of sin obvious; why then does man repeatedly embrace sin?
- Why are Christians so apparently open to teachings not supported in Scripture?
- Why are Christians so open to being deceived?

Refreshingly, this book captures Elder Robert methodically probing his way through these and other questions. While it is the responsibility of Elder Hill to reveal through this book the answers to the questions, I simply note for the reader that, in the end, he successfully points us back to the simple message of the Bible: Jesus is *"the"* door to salvation; Jesus is the answer.

Having read the early and final drafts, I commend Elder Hill for the introspective journey he traveled. To be honest, the questions he addresses are the questions I am often challenged with by seekers, new converts, and ministers in training to answer. The fact that he is especially gracious in sharing the answers to the questions as they emerged to him during his journey of self-probing should be reassuring to students and teachers.

Pastor Gerald Seals
Living Word Church & Fellowship
25 Blue Bird Trail
Irmo, SC 29063

Dedication

AFTER COMPLETING my doctoral experience, I declared to myself that I would not read or write for quite awhile. I was thoroughly exhausted. Yet, it seemed that the Holy Spirit took hold to my entire being the next day and marked this point in my spiritual history with intense prayer, meditation, and writing. It was during this intense experience that (I prayed, meditated, and wrote without becoming hungry or sleepy for days, or desired interaction with the natural world, and had to force my self to eat and sleep) I realized God was at work.

Following this most intense experience, God spoke and he called me to be a witness and minister unto him. At this most auspicious time in my history, he impressed upon me the theme of my ministry: deception in the body of Christ. During this time, I was also inspired to write this Book. Oddly, when I first sat down to write, I was so overwhelmed with what the Spirit was saying, with all my thoughts, and all I had read, I could not write at all. Approximately two years later when I sat down to do an outline, this book flowed.

After I had completed this book and was in the process of editing for perfection, the Holy Spirit asked me: "will this book save souls?" Smiling, I said "surely thou knowist." Father, it is my desire that you be glorified and souls saved. Accordingly, Father God, I dedicate this book to you! Thank you God for the many revelations, resilience, and strength you gave me to make this book a reality.

Preface

THE CAUSE of man's perpetual apostasy and spiritual failure from the Dispensation of Innocence to the Dispensation of Grace presents an intriguing question for examination. It is my primal assumption that these failures are the effects of human imperfections evolving from man's iniquitous birthright, sin. Thus, the purpose of this writing is to examine and understand man's iniquitous nature in the context of biblical and secular history. This approach will attempt to reveal all the actors on the stage of life, including Satan, that participate in deception, sin, and destruction of humanity.

I have also advanced the assumption that man's failure has much to do with his lack of knowledge and understanding of the orthodox word of God, as well as biblical and secular history. A resolve of the question "why" necessarily calls for an examination of man's impenitent ignorance and his willful rejection of God and His word.

I believe that a confluence of many factors contributes to man's described failure. A most compelling reason, however, is man's failure to perfect an intimate relationship with God. Neither has he understood what happened at the beginning of time and why Satan has such vitriolic hatred for God, Jesus Christ, the Holy Spirit, and God's creation.

Equally as relevant, man has not understood Satan's ploys of deception and the subtle and stealthy introduction of heretical doctrine into Christianity. This has been accomplished by Satan's use of the agency of secular government, and the invasion of institutionalized Churches of God by false prophets, preachers, teachers and brethren.

Paul, having studied the phenomenon of deception, made very clear in 2 Corinthians 11:3 that he feared man's mind would be corrupted from the simplicity that is in Christ. I too have come to understand that the mind is the battlefield where Satan plays out his ploys of deception. No matter how simplistic or complex in design, Satan's ploys of deception involves a skill-set that has been perfected down through the ages and should not be taken lightly.

I present herein a proactive (how to) approach to expose Satan's attack on the mind, intellect, and sensorial faculties of believers and non-believers. This involves in part the process of dialectics; a mental process engaged through cognitive abilities of the mind and verbal exchange. The total process is neurolinguistic dialectics, engaged through the cognitive domain (mind and senses), which is successful when focused on the mind of one who is susceptible and/or impressionable, and weak in faith.

Principle outcomes of neurolinguistic dialectics are doubt and chaos, mental impressions and expressions that are negative in content. These manifest in the form of a question, unbelief, distrust, and indecision.

It is not suggested or implied that the anticipated lessons learned from this book will provide an all inclusive panacea to defeat the enemy. Hopefully, it will provide a practical perspective to discern that man is the enemy's intended target of exploitation and destruction. To this end, I sought to present a practical approach that unveils the mystery of the enemy's tactics to entice the believer by deception and cause him to sin.

Notwithstanding, man has a major role here because sin is volitional and works to estrange man from God. Additionally, once sin is finished, it will bring forth death (Jas 1:15). The ultimate end here is death of the spirit, soul, and body, and eternal separation from God.

God created man with the propensity to do either good or sin. This power of choice is the ultimate expression of liberty God desired for all his created beings. This book will hopefully inform man that it is his exercise of the power of choice to sin that gives Satan the opportunity to advance his attack. The lifestyle we chose has much to do with whether we do good or sin.

Nevertheless, we must always be conscious that the line between a spiritual lifestyle and secular ways of living may become blurred at any time. With this caveat to be conscious of our behavior, hopefully God will be glorified and souls will be saved by this book.

Acknowledgments

I EXTEND profound gratitude and appreciation to the following persons for their support, encouragement, and shared dispositions of excellence. They all engaged me with robust discussion and discourse of God's word with great passion, profundity, and from varied perspectives. Moreover, they are all about the business of savings souls.

Pastor Gerald Seals, preacher and teacher, business owner, Management Professor, prolific writer, published author, and research enthusiast.

Pastor James P. Neal, preacher and teacher, truth seeker, recipient of the Peabody Award for being founder and host of a television documentary and magazine program, business owner, entrepreneur, Professor, avid reader and researcher, writer, and published author.

Pastor Clifton Sanford, my spiritual father who taught me the word of God from milk to meat for over 10 years by Faith-Love-Obedience-Worship, preacher and teacher, my mentor, entrepreneur, and fisherman by hobby.

Reverend Richard Crayton, preacher and teacher, entrepreneur, and Professor, who admonished me not to wait too long to heed the call of God, and who passionately desires to establish evangelistic works focused on teens to help them seek, learn, know, and embrace Christ as Lord and Savior.

Minister Phyllis Clyburn, preacher and teacher, published author of several books, nurse, and entrepreneur.

A very special thanks to my brother, Dr. Clarence W. Hill, a man of God, Professor, business owner, entrepreneur, and prolific writer and researcher, and my entire God-loving family for their support and passionate desire for my success.

Introduction

Humanity has been estranged from God since the fall of Adam and Eve in the Garden of Eden. Since the great fall, humanity has experienced five and one-half dispensations of the ages of time established by God.[1] Each dispensation, from Innocence to Law, concluded with apostasy and utter failure induced by deception. It was by deception that humanity was estranged from God. Thus, deception has been and remains one of the dominant, persistent, and provocative threats to the Body of Christ throughout church history. Notwithstanding, God has endeavored to reconcile humanity, Jew and gentile, to himself from eternal separation and death to eternal life.

One could easily assume that the Dispensation of Grace, which believers are now experiencing, will end like the previous ages of time. This assumption emanates from a tenable position that man and his institutions now exist in a culture of corruption, a sinful state-of-being that is pathologically diseased. In this regard, man has not evolved much from this terminal state-of-being inherited from the Garden of Eden experience.

Giving due consideration to man's iniquitous ways and failures, God continues to woo and succor him to a reconciled relationship. God's desire for reconciliation was first established with the Old Testament Biblical Sacrificial System, and presently through the advent of New Testament

Soteriology. Soteriology, consisting of the Doctrine of Salvation and other promises of God, is perhaps the grandest theme in scripture and greatest works of God.

Salvation was perfected by God to provide mankind a personal, direct, and volitional means to escape total eternal separation and damnation and receive eternal life. The Doctrine of Salvation centers on the personage of an awesome savior, Jesus Christ, and comprehends a substitutionary sacrifice, redemption, righteousness, justification, sanctification, and propitiation.

Given God's well established and persistent intent to reconcile humanity to himself, the question becomes: why has humanity replicated the same negative behavior age after age regressing to the same inevitable results of apostasy and failure? There are perhaps many human imperfections that contribute to these results. To be considered is man's iniquitous nature coupled with his inability to understand spiritually how the innate flaw of human imperfection called sin effects human behavior and salvation.

There is also the failure to understand what happened at the beginning of time, and why Satan has such vitriolic hatred for God, Jesus Christ, the Holy Spirit, and all of God's creation. Another compelling exemplar is man's failure to perfect an intimate relationship with God; or hear and follow the voice of his Sheppard (John 10:27); or perhaps he is not submitted to his pastor and does not embrace the rule of subjection (Heb 13:17) and (Rom 13:1–2).

I would suggest that the confluence of others factors such as sorrow, tragedy, misery, grief, social, political, and economics have contributed to man's continued failure down through the ages. I would strongly suggest, however, that one primal reason is man's iniquitous birthright (Ps 51:1–17). This is no less than sin-*hamartia*-or missing the mark (Rom 3:23).[2]

The purpose of this writing is to examine and understand man's iniquitous nature in the context of biblical and secular history, and discover the wiles and schemes employed by Satan to induce deception, sin, and destruction of humanity. Perhaps this approach will help believers and non-believers understand their own basic nature, rightly divide scripture, and discern the full counsel of God's word and attendant knowledge.

It is clear from the dynamics played out in the Garden of Eden through the 1st Millennium post-Pentecost to present that Satan intends eternal destruction and damnation of humanity-spirit, soul and body-and all of God's creation. The means (wiles and schemes) he uses to accomplish this varies.[3] He uses in part a false prophet, teacher, a spurious apostle, pretended preacher, and/or false teacher), all who subtly and stealthily introduce heretical doctrines denying God (2nd Pet 2:1).[4] He also uses the agency of secular government, as well as institutionalized Churches of God to achieve his intended end.

Many will follow these false prophets and teachers, who will make merchandise (exploit) of you (2nd Pet 2:3). The many that will follow these false prophets, teachers, spurious or false brothers, and even pretended associates are described by God as rebellious people and lying children (Isa 30:9). They say to seers, see not; and to the prophet, prophesy not unto us right things, speak smooth things or smoothness of the tongue, prophesy deceit (Isa 30:10).

False prophets and teachers, and false brethren are among those who employ acts of deception to deceive God's people. These are they who are heretics and will destroy the church, and deny the existence of the Father, Son, and Holy Spirit (1st John 2:18, 22). These are also they who will go out from among us making it plain that they are not believers (1st John 2:19). This is descriptive of the great apostasy or falling away.

Reiterating, man's apostasy and failure throughout the ages has been the sequela of deception, the favored tool of destruction and damnation used by Satan against Adam and Eve in the Garden of Eden. He has been using this tool ever since.

In the Second Epistle of Corinthians, Paul was concerned about the saints being exposed to doctrinal errors (heretical doctrines) and the disruption of his work by legalistic teachers. In this context, he addressed doctrinal errors and legalistic teachings that were being taught, and focused on the mind and intellect of saints. More specifically, Paul stated in 2nd Cor 11:3: "But I fear, lest by any means, as the serpent beguiled Eve through his subtlety, so your mind should be corrupt from the simplicity that is in Christ."[5] In addition to the vulnerability of the mind, intellect, and sensorial susceptibility of believers to deception, there is another component to the process of deception that is clearly demonstrated in Gen 3:1-6. This is the process of dialectics.

Dialectics has been used by the enemy down through the ages as a major means to deploy deception. Dialectics is a mental process engaged through cognitive abilities of the mind and verbal exchange. Hence, the mind is the battlefield where this neurolingusitic process is used to instigate deception and is played out.

At play on the battle field is another component of dialectics just as essential as the mind. This is the tongue. While this is a little member of the body, it is in and of itself wicked, a fire, evil, and can not be tamed (Jas 3:5–8). In the context of dialectics, the tongue is used to facilitate communication of thoughts and ideas spoken to corrupt the mind and beliefs of a listener who is susceptible and/or impressionable.

Satan's strategy for success requires that he focus the ploy of deception on a believer's spirit, soul, and body. The strategy typically begins in a subtle, stealthy manner, which is asserted gradually and imperceptibly by varying means. Generally, the means deployed to begin the ploy of deception involves neurolinguistic dialectics, as used in the Garden of Eden; a process engaged through the cognitive domain (mind and senses) and perfected by verbal exchange. Neurolinguistic dialectics is successful when focused on the mind of a believer who is susceptible and/or impressionable, and weak in faith. Reiterating, the venue and battlefield of deception is the mind.

In order to defeat deception and sin, we must understand the origin and process of dialectics, as well as how the enemy operates. The human mind and sensorial faculties of sight, smell, hearing, taste, and touch are in effect composite neurolinguistic attributes through which the dialectic process is actualized. One of the principle outcomes of neurolinguistic dialectics is doubt; a mental expression, negative in content, that manifest in the form of a question, unbelief, distrust, and indecision.

Doubt typically evolves from the lack of faith in God and His power to perform his word by keeping his promises and oaths. From the beginning of time to present, God knew that man could and would be deceived. Deception exists in and outside the church and assembly. By virtue of his omniscience, God also knew the day would come when man would attempt to change his purpose, precepts, word, law, time, and order by deception.

It was for this reason too that Paul admonished us to ". . . be no more children, tossed to and fro, and carried about with every wind of doctrine, by the sleight of men and cunning craftiness (cunning, cleverness of unscrupulous men in every sifting form of trickery) whereby they lie in wait to deceive (Eph 4:14). As we attempt to disaggregate and understand deception, sin, and neurolinguistic dialectics, we must be mindful of and address several fundamental questions:

> What is sin and its origin?
> What is deception and its origin?
> Who deploys acts of deception?
> What is dialectics?
> What is neurolinguistic dialectics?
> What are the outcomes of neurolinguistic dialectics?

In no wise is it suggested or implied that the anticipated lessons learned from this piece will provide an all inclusive panacea to defeat or destroy the enemy. Hopefully, it will show that no matter how simplistic or complex in design, the enemy's ploys of deception involves a skill-set that has been perfected down through the ages and should not be taken lightly.

It is anticipated that believers and unbelievers will receive a practical perspective that will enable them to discern that they are the enemy's intended target of exploitation and destruction. This perspective brings into focus the realization that sin gives access (an open door) to the enemy, and once sin is finished, it will bring forth death (Jas 1:15). Sin is volitional and it works to estrange man from God.

Ultimately, this level of discernment will help expose the enemy's predictable course of action(s) or inaction(s) designed to cause believers to roam from safety and truth, and be deceived. This approach will also help defeat believer's self-deception, ignorance of the enemy's schemes and ploys, and erroneous presumptions about the enemy that are self-defeating. A form of ignorance that is just as harmful pertains to the "lack of knowledge of God" and the rejection of God from human activities.

The lack of knowledge of God and the rejection of God equates to sin and ultimately a lawless society; one that is morally bankrupt, irreverent, ignorant (unlearned about God and His righteousness because man rejected Him) spiritually debased. Without requisite knowledge of God and biblical and secular history, humanity will remain alienated from God, and his understanding will be darkened and his heart blinded. This behavior, uncorrected, will once more lead to utter failure of humanity, and the Dispensation of Grace will end like the previous ages of time.

1

The Mystery of Our Perfect God the Creator and the Paradox of a Perfect Creation Who Committed Sin

MAN HAS been baffled by God since the beginning of time, endeavoring to understand his mysterious nature and character. God has been, is, and remains a mystery to most, save those of his elect. The mysteries or hidden things of God and his kingdom were kept secret from the beginning of the world, but have been revealed to God's elect by God directly (Col 1:27), through the teachings of Jesus Christ (Rom 16:25), the Holy Spirit (Eph 6:19)(1st Cor 2:10), the prophets (Rom 16:26), by revelation (Eph 3:3), and the reading of His word (Eph 3:4).

Notwithstanding, even for us who believe, we only know in part (1st Cor 13:9). Our expectancy is that . . . when that which is perfect is come, then that which is in part shall be done away (:10). This result can only attain when one turns to Jesus Christ, having accepted him as Lord and Savior. At this point, the veil of spiritual ignorance as to wisdom and knowledge of God and his mysteries is lifted and the process of spiritual transformation commences . . . (2nd Cor 3:12–16). While things not revealed belong unto the Lord our God, those things which are revealed belong to us and our posterity forever, that we may do all the words of this law (Deut 29:29).

These secret things were historically known as sacred secrets, the hidden things, but are contemporarily referred to as revealed secrets.[1] This is consistent with Ephesians 1:9 which states that God "made known" to us the mystery of His will according to his good pleasure which he hath purposed in himself. Having made known to us his sacred secrets is the equivalency of "revealed secrets." Sacred secrets or revealed secrets means a secret in the spiritual realm that God only knows, and can only be made known by him. What God only knows is outside natural apprehension and must be made known by spiritual revelation.

Among the most profound mysteries man has pondered is "Why God created man"? Some even inquire "What is man that God would consider him at all or even visit him" as did David in Ps 8:4. More importantly, who is man that God continuously tolerate his sinful ways? And who is man that God would exalt him still in the Kingdom of God?

God created man in his image—nature and character— and likeness (Gen 1:26 and 27) to be God-centered, the center of all things in the earth, His Vice Regent, but not anthropocentric.[2] God intended that man, as a perfectly created spirit being would have a spiritual and personal relationship with him, an eternal love and not an ephemeral affair, and an eternal life. Thus, man's raison d'etre, his sole purpose for being or his highest ultimate aim was and remains to glorify God himself and enjoy him for an eternity.

In Aramaic language, the image of God is Tzelem Elokim, which translates in meaning to a mold, affirming that humankind was created in the "image' of God.[3] Thus, man is the image and glory of God (1st Cor 11:7), which is representative of God. In Hebraic language the word image is translated tzelem, meaning a mold.[4] This mold provided the archetype of a perfect man, Adam, and all of humanity—*ha'Adam*—that would follow his creation; yet, no two beings are alike.

The expression "in the image of God" depicts man as a liberated and intelligent being just as God his creator. In effect, God was not just creating another image, but an image of himself. As to his likeness, this depicts man walking out his life's destiny, moving progressively towards the attainment of God's image. The object of this journey can only be attained through the synergy (team work) of man and the Holy Spirit. The process of cooperation is what we call theosis, man's transformation into the likeness and union with God by the power of the Holy Spirit.

As we inquire of God and His mysteries, we discover that He created the Mystery of Good and the Mystery of Iniquity or Lawlessness. It would appear that these diametrically opposing qualities or attributes created by a perfect God presents an unintended and/or an unexplained paradox. Why would our perfect God the Creator create a perfect creation—man—with the propensity to do both good and sin?[5] Can a perfect man sin? If man sins, is he perfect?

An examination of what is seemingly a paradox requires one to remember that God is Holy and sovereign; the well-spring of his unequivocal perfection, goodness, and power.[6] It is in the context of perfection, goodness, and power he made clear in Isaiah 45:7 that: "He form the light and created darkness." He said "I make peace and create evil: I the Lord do all these things." However, while God is himself at all times good and created evil, he did not sin or commit evil. Again, he is Holy with moral perfection and ethical purity, and everything he created is perfect and pure and complete, including man.

In his sovereignty and comprehensiveness, God is the sum and irreducible substance of all there is, was, and is to come. All things consist and persist of God. All things were made by him, and without him was not any thing that was made (John 1:3). None of God's attributes of perfection are independent of or preeminent over any of the others, and he is at all times greater than the sum of all his attributes. Thus, when we consider the attributes and comprehensiveness of God, remember: we still have not adequately or fully described him (John 21:25).

These attributes of perfection are inherent in God's creation. This is so with man, for he was created perfect-*tamiym*-without spot and undefiled, but with the innate -though dormant- propensity to sin. We must remember that in the context of God's perfect creation, man, there is imperfection existing at all times. Man was created a free moral agent seized of divine right by God with the liberty to exercise the prerogative of choice: to do good or to sin. This is indicative of man's liberty and his power of choice.

The power of choice is known in Hebrew idiomatic expressions as the idiom of permission.[7] Expressed differently, God gave man permission to do good or sin. The responsibility for committing sin rest in the created. Therefore, God did not sin, even though he created sin as expressed in Isaiah 45:5–7.

The imperfection of sin presents what would seemingly be a paradox in that our perfect God the creator created a perfect creation in Adam who committed sin. The contemporary definition and usage of the word perfect varies from the Hebrew word *tamiym*, which comprehends man's innate propensity to sin. Hence, there is no paradox. Perfect in the Hebrew means nothing need be added or taken away. It also mean spiritually mature, upright, whole, blameless, undefiled, and flawless.

These descriptors of perfection are imputed to man by God. Thus, perfection, which also includes the propensity to sin, contemplates moving from the propensity to sin- *tamiym*- to actualized sin -*hamartia*. God is and remains perfect. It is this same perfection that inspired him to create a perfect man.

Whatever we call man's sinful conduct, it is sin. This is conduct evidencing man's failure to stand the test or hit the mark, a standard of conduct established by God: e.g. the mark of righteousness, the mark of love, mark of obedience, or the mark of glorifying God. Sin is a state of being sufficient enough to effect eternal separation from God, and its penalty is spiritual, physical, and eternal death. Sin in the earth was found in the Garden of Eden, a place called delight.[8] This was man's first expression of his iniquitous nature in the earth.

It was through Adam's sin that sin entered this world, and was imputed to all of humanity.[9] However, the first known instance or origin of sin was not in the earth but in heaven. It was Lucifer, an anointed cherub, who sinned first and whose iniquitous conduct is first recorded in Isaiah

14:5: He, Lucifer, was perfect in his creation "until iniquity was found in him."

By Jesus Christ . . . were all things created, that are in heaven, and that are in earth, visible and invisible, whether [they be] thrones, or dominions, or principalities, or powers: all things were created by him, and for him: (Col 1:16). This included the creation of Lucifer, the premiere covering cherub, holy and undefiled.

Lucifer, whose name means brilliant star or morning star or light bearer was a created being (Ezk 18:15) who existed among angels, the first known beings created by God.10 His task was to serve God. As an angle, he was a mortal being (Luke 20:36); yet, uniquely created as a pre-eminent anointed cherub (Ezk 18:14). Specifically, God created Lucifer as an expression of his own perfect beauty and power (Ezk 28:12–15).

Lucifer was full of wisdom and beauty (Ezk 18:12). His physical angelic being consisted of every precious stone and with tabrets and pipes to fulfill his Godly purpose for being: to create music (Ez k 28:13).[11] He was perfect and blameless from the time of his creation, until iniquity was found in him (:13–15).[12]

As to his station and role in the grand scheme of heaven and earth, Lucifer led the worship of the universe in the presence of God and did shine the light of glory on God. He was the chief guardian of God's holiness and majesty. God also created him to inhabit the earth. This included the Garden of God spoken of in Ezk 28:13. He had access to Heaven and the Holy Mount of God (:14), believed to have been a physical mountain created on earth from which Lucifer ruled the nations in his charge.

When Lucifer resolved to sin, it was deliberate with the intent to corrupt the holy character of godliness with which God had endowed him and all his creation (Ezk 28:12–17). Lucifer's deliberative intent was clearly established when he declared his five idolatrous "I wills" as stated in Isaiah 14:13–14:

> I will ascend into heaven, I will exalt my throne above the stars of God: I will sit also upon the mount of the congregation, in the sides of the north: I will ascend above the heights of the clouds; I will be like the most High.

Though Lucifer was the epitome of perfection, God now viewed him -post sin- as a profane thing (Ezk 28:16), whose iniquitous character derived from a proud heart inspired by his beauty, and corrupted wisdom inspired by his splendor (:17). Expressed differently, Lucifer's power and beauty collaborated with his authority and privileges to inspire sin.

Lucifer's unholy aspirations to be like the most high God in his divinity, sovereignty, and superior knowledge was inspired by pride and the desire for God's glory. With these godly attributes, Lucifer thought he could ascribe unto himself the personification of god. This unholy aspiration to be like the most high was flawed ab-initio. Where would Lucifer acquire the power, presence, and knowledge to affect a successful coup against God, his creator. Nevertheless, he now knows as a lesson learned, as does all of heaven and humanity, that none can be like the most high God, El Elyon. Thus, he could never be exalted above God.

God did cast Lucifer out of the Mountain of God because of his iniquitous behavior, and further resolved to not only cast him to the earth (Ezk 28:17), but to expose him by laying him out for display before kings to see, and eventually destroy him (See Isa 14:9–12). God did not view Satan's ouster from heaven as a particularly good thing for humanity, saying in Revelations 12:12:

> Woe to the inhabiters of the earth and of the sea for the devil comes down unto you, having great wrath, because he knoweth that he hath but a short time.

In his fallen state, Lucifer is known as Satan. This means accuser as in the story of Job, and/or deceiver as in the case of Adam and Eve. One can only question whether Lucifer's unholy aspiration—to be like God—was worth being separated from the presence of God.

Lucifer was created a perfect physical being by God, but morally imperfect. The mystery of iniquity manifested in him because God created him, as Adam, with the prerogative of choice: to choose good or to sin. This innate propensity to sin, manifested unequivocally when Lucifer, the created, choose to rebel against God. As a God-created being possessed with the innate ability to sin, the responsibility for committing sin was his as one who had the liberty to exercise the power of choice: to do good or to sin

This matter of choice reflects another aspect of God's unique creation of Lucifer. He possessed the cognitive ability to know, think, reason, and make decisions. He was distinguished from other angles in that they were yielded, submitted, and attentive to God's will, except for the third of the angelic host that rebelled against God following Lucifer (2nd Pet 2:4)(Rev 12:4).

Adam was made in the image and likeness of God. He too was made perfect and a free moral agent by God, seized of right with the prerogative of choice; to choose good or to sin. God's intentions toward man, as a perfectly created spirit being, manifested fully in the Garden of Eden where He gave man purpose: to dress the garden (Gen 2:15), and exercise dominion over all the earth and all things (Gen 2:26). This God given purpose included the implicit command to occupy and watch the Garden of Eden.

Adam and his God created and given wife (Eve) were created innocent, having no consciousness of sin. Knowing no sin. Adam's sin manifested after he and Eve were respectively deceived and beguiled by Satan, and ate of the tree of knowledge of good and evil contrary to the will of God.[13] Adam's failure to achieve God's purpose is the first demonstration of human imperfection, sin, by man in the earth.

This single act of sin and/or transgression by Adam (and Eve) known as the great fall, was imputed to all of humanity, who have remained estranged from God. This single act of sin is also the seminal reason for man's iniquitous birthright (depraved, perverted and sinful) (Ps 51:1–17). Additionally, this single act of sin provided the impetus for Adam and Eve to be sent away from the Garden of Eden; for terminating the Dispensation of Innocence and initiated the Dispensation of Consciousness (to know good and evil); and commencing the process of physical and eternal death.[14]

During the Dispensation of Innocence and the Edenic Covenant, Adam and Eve were both pure in spirit and body, untested by temptation, and received covering directly from God. Neither did they have knowledge of good or evil, nor self-consciousness. Thus, there was no need for salvation until the great fall, which led to the Dispensation of Consciousness.

2

Deception and Its Evolution in the Body of Christ

SOME OF the more dominant themes of the twenty-first century are change, uncertainty, intolerance, pessimism, technological advancement, and exponential expansion of knowledge. There are also wars and rumors of wars, a new world order inclusive of a one world religion, as well as an indifference and lack of compassion for human beings. These themes are foundational for a new and growing post-church era celebrated as New Age Apostasy that flourishes in what is known as the Emerging Church. This genre of churches thrives on deception designed to undo faith in believers, and destroy the orthodox church of God. The operative word here is deception, which has existed throughout Church history.

Since the era of Adam and Eve, humanity has experienced five (5) and one-half of six dispensations of the ages of time established by God. Each dispensation, from Innocence to Law, concluded with apostasy (delusion and deception/falling away from truth), and utter failure. This is from the "Great Fall of Adam" to the "Falling Away" (apostasy) of the church. The described themes of the twenty-first century strongly suggest that the Dispensation of Grace, which humanity is now experiencing, will conclude in the same manner.

The issue to be resolved is why man has replicated the same negative behavior age after age regressing to the same inevitable result? It is believed that the resolve of this issue exist in establishing a relationship with God, understanding the word of God which comes by rightly dividing his word, and understanding human behavior in the context of biblical and secular history.

There are perhaps many human imperfections that contribute to apostasy and utter failure. For instance, there is the failure to understand what happened at the beginning of time, and why Satan has such vitriolic hatred for God, Jesus Christ, the Holy Spirit, and all of God's creation. Other compelling exemplars are man's failure to perfect an intimate relationship with God; or hear and follow the voice of his Shepard (John 10:4); and perhaps man has not submitted to a pastor and does not embrace the rule of subjection (Heb 13:17)(Rom 13:1–2).

It is strongly suggested, however, that one primal reason for man's continued failure is his imputed iniquitous birthright, of which Adam is the progenitor. This can be summed up in one word, sin or *hamartia*.[1] To be considered also is man's inability to understand spiritually how sin influences and changes human behavior.

Not pretermitting the plausible explanations for apostasy and failure as delineated, it is suggested that the confluence of many other factors, e.g. sorrow, tragedy, misery, grief, social, political, and economic, have contributed to man's continued failure down through the ages.

A more contemporary perspective informs us that man and his institutions now exist in a culture of corruption; a sinful state-of-being that is pathologically diseased. Some would even question whether we have arrived at that point in time where it can be said "As it was in the days of Noe . . . (Matt 24:36–39; Luke 17:26–27), and whether we have truly stepped into the Loadicean Era as a church (Rev 3:14–22).

The above stated suggestions as to possible causes of apostasy and utter failure are not to say that man has not progressed spiritually or is incapable of godly and holy behavior. Yet, the explication of man's behavior is to emphasize that the dominant themes of the twenty-first century are consistent with those of the Adam and Eve era. These themes are deception, sin, and failure. Even so, God has allowed man to remain the same as he was created in the beginning: a perfect free moral agent seized of divine right by God with the liberty to exercise the prerogative of choice.[2] That is to do good or to sin.

God's attributes of perfection comprehends imperfection, the innate propensity to sin. In spite of his apostasy and utter failure, God has not removed or diminished man's cognitive abilities (to know, think, reason, and make decisions) and liberty associated with the power of choice.

Where has the Christian Church evolved in today's culture and society, and what circumstances and conditions impact those who are called out by God? Principally, the Christian Church now exist in an emerging Post-Modernistic Era where there is no absolute truth to agree on, and principals and doctrines of old do not work any more. These are the more generalized circumstances and conditions that give rise to apostasy, and institutions such as the contemporary Emerging Church.

Apostasy, the departure or turning away from God's truth, is also rampart because people want to hear smooth things and not sound doctrine from the pulpit (Isa 30:10). False preachers and teachers are dispensing such false doctrine out of their own wisdom and revelation. Perhaps these preachers and teachers have failed to read and rightly divide God's word, or intentionally preach and teach a gospel different from God's word. Either circumstance is a true source of apostasy devised by those whom God considers to be profane and lying things (Ezk 22:26–29).

There are numerous other popular doctrines embraced by wavering believers. Some have embraced the Replacement Theory believing that because Jews rejected and crucified Jesus Christ, God broke His Abrahamic Covenant and positioned the Christian Church as spiritual Israel endowed with all the original promises of Israel.[3]

There is also the Cessationists who assert the belief that charismatic gifts of the Holy Spirit, such as tongues, prophecy and healing ceased being practiced in early Church history.[4] Among the popular doctrines is a hew and cry for a New World Order that will eliminate YHWH as God and acknowledge a feminine deity-Gaia-as god.[5]

This New World Order embraces destruction of the family unit, national patriotism, and rights of private property. That which is good is now called bad, and vice-versa; there is Humanism that views man as the center and cause of his destiny without God; genetic engineering called cloning where beings will be created without a soul, who did not come into this earth through the matrix of a woman, and are forever bastards of this world; and the Doctrine of Preterism is being popularized, teaching that Jesus Christ has already fulfilled His promise to come again.

The described doctrines, circumstances, and conditions of today presents an impressive statement that supports the continuation of apostasy and failure of humanity in the twenty-first century. Apostasy and failure presents a formidable challenge to the Orthodox Church of God and individual believers. This formidable challenge is sustained through the works of the spurious apostle, pretended preacher, false teacher, brother, and pretended associate. They continue in their erroneous, deceitful ways to destroy the church by dissuading individual believers away from orthodox beliefs to what is known as New Age Apostasy.

God knew from the beginning of time that man could and would deceive and be deceived, and perish because of his very sin nature and character, which is evil, feeble, and frail. Jeremiah identified the locus of deception as the heart, saying: The heart is deceitful above all things, and desperately wicked and perverse, who can know it, perceive, understand, be acquainted with his own heart and mind (Jer 17:9). Timothy even went as far as to identify who will use and be the object of deception, saying: evil men and seducers shall wax worse, deceiving and being deceived (2nd Tim 3:13).

Notwithstanding, it is God's will that no man will perish (John 3:16), and that His elect shall be saved in the Lord with an everlasting salvation (Ish 45:17). There is, however, a condition precedent to everlasting salvation; that man believes on the Son of God. This is confirmed by Jesus who said that this is the will of him that sent me, that everyone which seeth the Son, and believe on him, may have everlasting life; and I will raise him up at the last day (See John 6:38-47).

While it is the will of God that all men be saved and have everlasting life, God will give lukewarm believers and unbelievers over to their reprobate minds (Rom 1:28). Such persons in the eyes of God are worthless and rejected, and spiritual death is the ultimate consequence of their unbelief (Rom 1:28–32). To those given to a reprobate mind, God will even mingled a perverse spirit among them, causing them to commit iniquity, be deceived and error in every work (Isa 19:14).

DECEPTION MADE REAL: UP CLOSE AND PERSONAL

Deception is a derivative of the word deceive, which is *planao* in Greek, meaning to cause to roam from safety, truth, or virtue; go astray, err, seduce, or be out of the way.[6] A related word is *plane*, which means fraudulent, straying from piety, delusion, error. The word deception is not a neologism, nor is it a subject for a new or one-time message to God's people. God has sought to get this message out on deception throughout the ages. It is not likely to inspire one to jump and leap for joy. Yet, God's message on deception is given to us to save souls.

This message on deception is about (1) growing and ignored error/sin/transgression/iniquity in the Body of Christ, and (2) God's offering of salvation through the love of truth for believers via teaching, preaching, prayers and supplication, and intercession for the believer and unbeliever. Thus, this messenger and writer must speak, howl or cry loud and spare not his voice in exposing deception (Is 58:1).

What this message requires of the messenger is to say unequivocally "What Thus Saith The Lord." This includes speaking truth to power as the Prophet Nathan spoke to

King David (2nd Sam 12:1–25), and to watch for and purge demons of deception from among saints and sinners, where ever they exist. Otherwise, man shall be condemned and howl himself for vexation of the spirit (See Ish 65:1–14).

Deployment of deception requires imagination, and it is an essential component of the mystery of iniquity or lawlessness (See 2nd Thess 2:7–10). It is Satan who works iniquity and deception in humanity, and he does so through false prophets, preachers, teachers, the brethren, and the Antichrist(s). It is Satan who will seek to accomplish iniquity with all (pretended) power and signs and lying wonders, and with all deceivableness of unrighteousness (wicked deception) in them that perish because they did not receive the love of the truth, that they might be saved.

Notwithstanding, we as the Christian Church and believers are encouraged to be mindful of Paul's revelation pertaining to deception and Satan in 2nd Cor 11:

> 12 But what I do, that I will do, that I may cut off occasion from them which desire occasion; that wherein they glory, they may be found even as we.
>
> 13 For such are false apostles, deceitful workers, transforming themselves into the apostles of Christ.
>
> 14 And no marvel, for Satan himself is transformed into an angel of light.
>
> 15 Therefore it is no great thing if his ministers also be transformed as the ministers of righteousness; whose end shall be according to their works.

3

God's Intentions and Admonitions Regarding Deception in the Body

It is God's intention to warn and save His elect from eternal destruction and death of the spirit, soul, and body. For this purpose, God sent his message in diverse ways (Rom 16:25 and 26) (Eph3:3–4 and 6:19); (1ˢᵗ Corin 2:10) and (Col 1:27), admonishing His elect to take heed that no man deceive you (Mat 24:4, 5, 24). This is because many false christs and false prophets will come in the name of Jesus Christ with the intent to deceive God's very elect. Thus, God's elect simply can not believe every spirit it encounters; yet, must try every spirit to discern whether they are of God (1ˢᵗ John 4:1).

It is for this cause, to warn and save His elect from destruction and death, that God sent his word eternal and everlasting, Jesus Christ, into this world. This mission was implemented when Jesus started His public ministry, then discipling 12 men who became Apostles, and by ministering the word of God to countless Jews and Gentiles. Second, this mission was established in perpetuity when Jesus Christ ascended from the pit of hell into heaven, interimly giving gifts to men (Ps 68:18)(Eph. 4:8): some apostle, some prophets, some evangelists, and some pastors and preachers (:11). These gifts were given for the perfecting of the saints, works of the ministry, and the edifying of the body of Christ (:12).

The mission to warn and save God's elect, and whosoever that will come, is to be realized by the set ministries appointed by God to facilitate building the Kingdom of God through service to God's saints. The expectation is that His people will come into the unity (oneness) of faith, knowledge of the Son of God, and mature in the measure of the statute of the fullness of Christ (See Eph. 4:11-13). There is also the Great Commission and ministry of reconciliation to be carried out, which devolves upon all God's elect, inclusive of the set ministries.

These things accomplished, God's people will be warned and saved from eternal destruction and death, and the enemy will not work his will in or upon the Body of Christ by any means of deception. This requires that God's people will heed His word. In this regard, apostles, prophets, evangelists, pastors and preachers must continue to teach and admonish believers as did Paul:

> That we henceforth be no more children, tossed to and fro, and carried about with every wind of doctrine, by the slight of men and cunning craftiness (cleverness of unscrupulous men in every shifting form of trickery) whereby they lie in wait to deceive (Eph 4:14).

WHAT THE ENEMY INTENDED BY DECEPTION

It is clear from the dynamics played out in the Garden of Eden to present that Satan intends eternal destruction and damnation of humanity, as well as the rest of God's creation. The means (wiles and schemes) by which he intends to accomplish this are varied. It may be to sift (test or tempt) you as wheat as Jesus informed Simon (Luke 22:31). He may come as a thief to steal, kill, and/or destroy the brethren (John 10:10), or even appear as your adversary feigning to be a roaring lion, walking about, seeking whom he may devour (1st Pet 5:8).

Another means may be as false prophets, teachers, or as a spurious apostle, who will subtly and stealthily introduce heretical doctrines denying God (2nd Pet 2:1). Many will follow these false prophets and teachers because they will defame the truth (2nd Pet 2:1). Moreover, with their covetousness (lust and greed) shall they with feigned words (cunning, false arguments) make merchandise (exploit) of you (2nd Pet 2:3).

The many who will follow false prophets and teachers are described by God in Isaiah as rebellious people and lying children (Isa 30:9). They say to the seers, see not; and to the prophets, prophesy not unto us right things, speak unto us smooth things meaning flattery or smoothness of the tongue or to prophesy deceits or even a delusion (Isa 30:10).

False prophets, teachers, and brethren are among those who will employ acts of deception and deceive God's people. These are they who are heretics and will destroy the church, and deny the existence of the Father, Son, and Holy Spirit (1st John 2:18–22).

These are also they who went out from among us making it plain that they are not believers (1st John 2:19). This is the great apostasy, or falling away. Reiterating, man's apostasy and failure throughout the ages has been the result of deception, the favored tool of destruction and damnation used by Satan against Adam and Eve in the Garden of Eden. He has been using this same tool every since.

Timothy addresses these matter, saying:

> Now the Spirit speaketh expressly, that in the latter times some shall depart from the faith, giving heed to seducing spirits, and doctrines of the devils; speaking lies in hypocrisy; having their consciousness seared with a hot iron (1st Tim 4:1–2).

Long before Timothy, Daniel spoke saying that:

> The day will come when the enemy will speak great words against the most High, and shall wear out the saints of the most High, and think to change times and laws (Dan 7:25).

4

The Beginning Church from Pentecost

MILLENNIAL HISTORICAL DEVELOPMENTS

SATAN HAS campaign for eternal destruction and damnation of humanity from the Dispensation of Innocence through Grace. Unlike his one-on-one direct capricious and deceptive appeal to Eve and Adam, Satan's appeal to humanity at the beginning of the Christian era was essentially through the agency of secular government and invasion of the institutionalized Church of God. His deluge against Christendom was and remains vitriolic and unrelenting, as evidenced by the varied schemes and devices of perversion used by him and his agents to defeat the Orthodox Church of God.

It was during the Feast of Pentecost at Jerusalem that the inclusive and universal Church of God came into being (Acts 1–2). This happened just as Jesus had promised the Apostles while on the earth: ". . . upon this rock I will build my Church and the gates of hell shall not prevail (stand) against it" (Mat 16:18).[1] Jesus' promise was fulfilled with the advent of the Holy Spirit, which gave birth to the Church (Acts 1:8). This was the beginning of the "One Holy Catholic and Apostolic Church."

Pentecost was the first act of God's Plan of Salvation for humanity following the ascension of Jesus Christ. The now spirit filled Apostles were greatly elevated in their spiritual consciousness, and the mystery of redemption had began. The Apostles were initially commissioned by Jesus (pre-ascension) to go only to the House of Israel (Mat 10:5–6). Post-ascension, they were commissioned by Him to go into all the world proclaiming the gospel, baptizing them in the name of the Father, Son and Holy Spirit, and teaching them all things He had commanded the disciples (Mat 28:17–20). This mission commenced on the day of Pentecost, when, through the Holy Spirit, the Church assumed its pre-ordained missionary character and role, which exist through to date (Act 2:1–47).

Pentecost is the day of an Old Testament Jewish festival that takes place on the fiftieth day of the Passover.[2] Pentecost is also known as the Feast of First Fruits (Exod 23:16) and the Feast of Weeks that comes seven weeks or week of weeks after the Feast of Passover (Deut 16:10). In the Jewish tradition, it is known as *"Shavout"*: celebrating the giving of the Torah at Mount Sinai and the birth of the Jewish Nation. Hence, Pentecost acquired the meaning of the fiftieth day.

As the focal event for the commencement and memorialization of Pentecost, Passover means more appropriately "protect" and not pass by or Passover with Jesus himself being the Passover sacrifice. Passover was instituted as a feast day to commemorate the Exodus of God's people out of bondage from Egypt (Exod 12), and His continued protection through the present. Passover is observed on the evening of the fifteenth of the Jewish calendar month Nisan.

This feast also commemorates God's extermination of all firstborn Egyptian males and beast. However, God spared the firstborn from death if he saw the blood of a sacrificial lamb on the doorpost and lintels of the house. Thus, passing over. The covering of doorposts with blood is also known as *kippur* in Hebrew.

Diverse people of different cultures and languages from all over the world came to Jerusalem during Pentecost to participate in the Old Testament celebration known as the Jewish harvest festival (Acts 2:5–12). Whether Jewish or converts to Judaism, they all came together with a shared common faith in God. They gave thanks to God for his many blessings, as well as gave offerings during the festival.

THE NEW TESTAMENT AND BEGINNING ORTHODOX CHURCH

The old festival known as Passover is now celebrated in tandem with New Testament activities that define Christian Pentecost. Pentecost comes as a result of the Holy Spirit's advent fifty days following the death and resurrection of Jesus Christ. This is also called the fiftieth day after Pascha, a Greek term which translates the Hebrew term Pesach for Passover. In this context, it is written: "For Christ, our paschal lamb, has been sacrificed" (1 Cor 5:7).

New Testament Pentecost recognizes that Jesus' death, burial and resurrection did take place, and that he was offered to God as the First Fruit among brethren from the dead (1 Cor 15:23). Pentecost also commemorates the outpouring of the Holy Spirit as the seminal event that gave birth to the Orthodox Catholic Church, which is headed by Jesus Christ.[3] The foundation of the Orthodox Church is premised on recognition of God the Father, Jesus Christ the head of the Church, and the Holy Spirit; the filling of Apostles and believers with the Holy Spirit; and the promise of salvation and eternal life to humanity.

The birth of the new Jewish nation came into being after the exodus from Egypt under the leadership of Moses, who transmitted to the people the Torah and Ten Commandments.

THE ORHODOX CHURCH

The word orthodox in the Greek means genuine and true and right believer, while Catholic in the Greek-katholikos- means universal. Noteworthy is that the original meaning of the orthodox Catholic Church differed greatly from its contemporary meaning, which will be addressed later.

At the beginning of the Orthodox Catholic Church in Jerusalem, it was the practice of the original Apostles to invite people of the Jewish faith to become Christians. This practice reflected Jesus' commission to the Apostles during his public ministry to preach and teach "only" to the House of Israel (Mat 10:5). This commission recognized that Jews were God's chosen people who believed in one true God, and who awaited a Messiah. This was evidenced in Acts 11:19, which shows disciples, following the persecution of Stephen, traveling as far as Phenice, Cyprus, and Antioch preaching to Jews only.

The scope of this ministry, however, was inconsistent with God's Plan of Salvation for an all inclusive universal Church. Jesus Christ changed this scope when he commissioned the Apostles to preach and teach the gospel world wide to all people (Mat 28:17–20).

The structure and administration of the beginning Church was very simple. Apostles were itinerate, who, after founding a new community of believers, appointed a stationary bishop to preside over the community. A priest and deacon were also appointed to assist in the administration of the word of God and Holy sacraments.[4] The Apostles were exclusively the original witnesses of Jesus Christ's public ministry and resurrection, commissioned by him to evangelize the world.

As new communities of believers were established, the described structure became the basic paradigm for God's inclusive and universal Orthodox Catholic Church.[5] Thus, the communities of believers were autocephalitic, self-contained and independent, all having in common One Father, One, Son, One Holy Spirit, One Word, and One Mission.[6]

CHRISTIAN PERSECUTION AND LIBERATION

Early believers and followers of Jesus Christ were first known as Jews, then as "Followers of the Way" (Acts 18:25; 19:9, 23; Acts 11:26).[7] The Followers of the Way were first called Christians at Antioch (Acts 11:26), and Christians were first called Catholics in a letter written by St. Ignatius of Antioch about the year 98–110 AD.[8] The Orthodox Church consisted of the original Christians or first Catholics from Pentecost, the original Apostles, and the new community of believers of the New Testament as they evolved.[9]

After the Church had established itself, believers were persecuted, scattered, and killed and sacred text, letters of Apostles, and temple structures were burned and destroyed.[10] Pharisees, Hellenist, Jews, the Roman Government, and heretics became chief antagonist of Christianity.[11] These groups were instrumentalities of Satan who sought to stymie and destroy Christianity by establishing Christo-paganism as a religion of the polytheistic Roman Empire.[12]

Christo-paganism was a religion of syncretism, blending and compromise instituted through the agency of Emperor Constantine and his perversion of the Orthodox Catholic Church of Rome.[13] Constantine, who declared himself priest and king, orchestrated the introduction of pagan rituals, practices and false doctrine into the Orthodox Church to displace Jesus Christ as head of the Church of Rome and his word.[14]

There were varied belief and value systems within Rome's cultural setting, such as the Sadducees, Hellenist, Jewish people, pagans and Christians. Notwithstanding, worship of the Roman Emperor "as god" was imposed upon all subjects of the Empire by Roman law.[15] This imposition placed Christians and Jews at odds with Roman Law because they too worshiped a single God (YHWH), and it was not the Roman Emperor. For this reason, the Roman government of that day did not trust Christians or Jews, or embrace their respective beliefs or value systems. From 66 to 70 AD, the Jewish State was destroyed and Christians were persecuted and killed for some 250 years.[16] These dynamics caused great conflicts in the lives and beliefs of believers.

During the first century, the Apostles wrote letters back and forth to each other and to various communities of believers. These letters or epistles were written by Paul,

James, John, and Jude. The four Gospels were also written by Matthew, Mark, Luke and John.

Early Christian beliefs were based on these apostolic teachings and preaching—*kerygma*—that were preserved and handed down in orthodox tradition and in New Testament scripture.[17] These writings, however, were subjected to multiple interpretations contrary to their orthodox meaning that had been passed down by the original Apostles. These unorthodox interpretations, e.g. the Doctrine of Arianism,[18] lead to major controversies in the Body of Christ and contributed to the introduction and incorporation of false doctrines and pagan practices into the Orthodox Christian Church.[19]

Satan knew he could not discourage or destroy the beginning Christian Church as a body of believers or individually by destroying sacred text or even temples. He knew it was the inerrant word of God, taught from early sacred writings and text of the Apostles now written on the heart, which inspired believers in their belief and missionary zeal. Satan had first hand knowledge of the power of the word of God, having been defeated by Jesus at the conclusion of his wilderness experience (Mat 4:4–10).

THE ROMAN EMPIRE AND RELIGION

Satan's next strategy was to stymie and then destroy the growth of Christianity by using organized Christo-paganism, the Roman state sponsored religion, as his main instrument of destruction. Through Constantine, Satan placed himself inside the Orthodox Church, empowering bishops to become pope (with self-ascribed papacy power) and the jurisdictional head of what would become the Roman Catholic Church. The pope also asserted self-ascribed deity, claiming power to speak as the vice regent of God on earth and exercise supreme authority over the Church and state. These self-ascribed "papal powers" caused an irreconcilable schism in the five ancient Christian patriarchates: Jerusalem, Antioch, Alexandria, Constantinople, and Rome.[20]

The birth of the Roman Catholic Church took place in the Roman Empire amidst the strongest and largest government on earth at that time. This Empire was too big and difficult for a single Emperor to manage. For this reason, in 286 AD, Roman Emperor Diocletian Antonianus divided the Roman Empire into east and west for administrative purposes, and ultimately established the Tetrarch (Rule of Four) in 293 AD.[21]

The Tetrarch System divided imperial power into a quadrumvirate (a divided imperial college of four regions), consisting of senior emperors with the title of "Augustus" and junior emperors with the title of "Caesar".[22] Emperor Diocletian was stationed in the east while Maximian, Diocletian's co-emperor, was stationed in the west. Galerius Maximanus and Flavius Valerius Constantius, also known as Constantius Chlorus, were chosen junior emperors stationed respectively in the east and west.

Once the original Apostles were dead, the Christo-pagan church started its emergence and the Orthodox Christian Church continued to grow and spread as well. In 303 AD, Emperor Diocletian called for the escalated persecution of Christian believers in order to stop this growth.[23] He viewed Christianity as a most formidable threat to the continued existence of the Roman Empire.[24] This view reflected a conviction that the effective strength of Christianity, its unstoppable exponential growth, and autonomous nature derived from the written word of God. Thus, he decreed and ordered that all sacred text and writings be destroyed. This action was also consistent with Diocletian's plan for homogeneity of religious ideas among diverse people and organizations under one Roman Empire.

Diocletian and Maximian abdicated their positions in 305 AD, and Constantius and Galerius were elevated in rank to Augusti, while Flavius Valerius Severus II and Constantine were respectively appointed junior emperors in the west and east.[25] These developments created chaos in subsequent years among those who would declare themselves Augusti or Caesar. This was because the Tetrarch System did not have a comprehensive plan or principles for succession. This was clear when Constantius died in 306 AD and his son Constantine, the succeeding heir, was declared emperor by the soldiers but was otherwise opposed.

In 312 AD, Constantine defeated Maxentius, son of Maximian at the Battle of the Milvian Bridge and became ruler of the entire Western Empire.[26] He then recognized Christianity as the "official religion" of Rome in 313 AD, declared himself head of the church, called for unification of all churches, and rejected practices of pagan worship.[27] The ancient Patriarchates, however, rejected his command for unification.

The persecution of Christians continued until 313 AD, when Emperor Constantine issued the Edict of Milan declaring Christianity a "state approved religion."[28] He too like Diocletian sought religious uniformity, but within the

Christian community. He even banished those who refused to comply and demanded that all property confiscated from the Church be returned. The Edict of Milan also set forth a policy of tolerance of religious diversity throughout the Empire.[29]

Thereafter, Constantine defeated Licinius, Emperor of the East, in 323 AD, and reunited east and west Rome and declared himself sole Augustus of the entire Roman Empire.[30] With this unification, he ended the Tetrarch System in 324 AD. For reasons of wealth and cultural strength of the eastern province of the Roman Empire, Constantine dedicated Constantinople, the Byzantine Empire, now present day Istanbul, Turkey, as New Rome in 330 AD and Headquarters of the Roman Empire.[31] It also became the center of Orthodox Christianity located in the east.[32]

The bishops of the great metropolitan centers, especially the Patriarch of Constantinople, were almost as powerful as the Emperor.[33] As the empire became increasingly autocratic, the church functioned *more* and more as an arm of the state. The Emperor's power grew absolute, and the Patriarch either pleased him or was deposed and replaced by someone more loyal.

ANCIENT PATRIARCHATES AND THE SCHISM

The community of Christian believers grew in to what was called the five ancient patriarchates (a system of five sees or administrations): four in the East and one in the West.[34] They were known collectively as the Pentarchy (Greek meaning five) consisting of Jerusalem, Antioch,

Alexandria, Constantinople, and Rome in the West, from which the Roman Catholic Church evolved.[35] Just as the beginning Church, each patriarchate was autonomous having jurisdiction over its own clergy and laity; yet, they were all united in faith, doctrine and sacraments as the "One Holy Catholic, Orthodox and Apostolic Church."[36]

Each patriarchate had an apostolic founder: Jerusalem had James in the Eastern Roman Empire; Antioch had Peter in the Eastern Roman Empire or Syria; Alexandria had Mark in the eastern Roman Empire or Egypt; Constantinople had Andrew in the Eastern Roman Empire or Istanbul, Turkey; and Rome had Peter and Paul in the Western Roman Empire.[37]

These five Churches, the Orthodox Catholic Church, maintained that they collectively and individually hold, preserve, and protect the original Church faith common to the East and West, as proclaimed by the original Apostles.[38] The faith of the original Church, which is inseparable from the orthodox tradition, is imbedded in the theological tradition practiced in the Eastern Mediterranean and Eastern European Church. These churches adamantly assert a distinguishing nature from all churches that are external to the ancient Pentarchy. Specifically, that they are keepers of the integrity of doctrine taught by the Original Apostles and subsequent church fathers.

While the Pentarchy comprises the One Holy Catholic, Orthodox and Apostolic Church, disagreements about ecclesiastical power and authority among the five churches caused an irreparable schism or split. This led to the Church of Roman separating and becoming the Roman Catholic Church. The actual split took place around 1054 AD,[39] and, thereafter, churches in the East referred to themselves as the Eastern Orthodox Church and the West referred to itself as the Roman Catholic Church. Historical developments of the Roman Catholic Church included the creation of what became known as papacy power.[40]

DEVELOPMENT AND POWER OF THE PAPACY

The Byzantine Church of the East, located in what Constantine designated as New Rome, was strongly identified with the Roman Empire as a state and national church.[41] It was more Greek in its linguistics and geography; yet, it kept the original orthodox doctrine and practices.[42] The linguistic orientation of the Church of Roman in the west was developed on the foundation of Latin culture.[43] While the Church of Rome maintained the original orthodox doctrine and practices, it recognized the Eastern Roman Church of Byzantine and its Holy See (dioceses or administration: the key unit of authority in the form of church governance known as episcopal polity) as illegitimate, and no more than a continuous rivalry.[44]

The Church in the west, headed by a bishop, was overly dependent upon Constantine for general protection and provisions. As overseer, the bishop assumed the onus for daily maintenance and survival of the Church in the west. The power and governance wielded by the Church was through a concept that became known as the papacy, which derives from the word papa or pope. Origin of the actual concept of papacy is not clear, but it did not exist before 130 AD.

Generally, the papacy comprehended a single office consisting of a bishop who presides over secular Rome, and a pope who presides over the ecclesiastical government of the Church of Rome. Both positions were vested in one person. Ecclesiastical and secular contributions to the concept's early development were numerous. Significant among ecclesiastical developments of the Church of Rome were the following self-ascribed attributes.[45]

Peter was declared to be the first bishop of Rome, and the Pope was deemed to be the successor of Peter. Thus, the Pope was viewed as the infallible representative of God with the right to define dogma and bind the consciousness of believers. Invocation of the Doctrine of Petrine Supremacy recognized the Pope as having universal authority over all bishops, and universal leadership over all churches.[46] The Bishop of Rome was conferred the authority to teach and interpret scripture and be called "Doctor of the Church" (teacher from the Latin word docere, to teach);[47] Yet, all bishops were viewed as equal in status but the Papacy claimed primacy of position among bishops, *primus inter pares*, and Rome itself was declared the seat of authority.[48]

THE IRRECONCILABLE CONTROVERSY

The self-ascribed attributes of the papacy created an irreconcilable controversy among all believers of the Orthodox Catholic Church, emphasis added as to members of the Patriarchates. This controversy was further aggravated when Emperor Theodosius the Great, in 380 AD, declared the Bishop of Rome as being the keeper of the true faith and supreme authority, and the Catholic Church of Rome as the sole legitimate imperial religion of the Empire.[49]

These secular declarations introduced another fissure in the ever widening breach between the members of the Patriarchy and Church of Rome. If these declarations had been accepted by the Patriarchates, their autocephalitic existence would have ended immediately and the Church of Rome would have exercised total control over all orthodox churches and believers.

These secular declarations were also an affront to the prevailing beliefs and practices of the orthodox believers who adamantly maintain even to day (1) they hold, preserve, and protect the original Church faith common to the East and West, as proclaimed by the original Apostles, and (2) they are keepers of the integrity of doctrine taught by the Original Apostles and subsequent Church fathers.[50]

During the 4th and 5th Centuries, papal power was significantly emboldened by Roman Emperors Constantine and Theodosius who decreed Christianity as the sole legitimate imperial religion of the Empire and the Bishop as having supreme authority.[51] The papacy started to freely wield political power in the west, using these decrees of apparent supreme authority, though vague, to exercise governance over secular and ecclesiastical matters of Western Rome.

The impetus for papal involvement in secular matters was the power vacuum created by Constantine's relocation of the Roman Empire's Headquarters from Western Rome to Constantinople. The Bishop eventually became the secular ruler of the City of Rome because the Roman Empire of the East failed to provide an imperial presence in the form of economic, political and military support for the City.[52]

Bishops were also encouraged to preserve the culture of Rome being defiled by undesired assimilating aliens.[53]

The presence of aliens resulted from successive conquering barbarian tribes that all but vitiated the power of the Church of Rome, the only true power in the west. This was the corollary of Constantine's relocation of the Roman Empire's Headquarters; a power vacuum in Western Rome that barbarian tribes sought to fill by wars and invasions. Typical of the wars fought against Western Rome was the Visigoths (meaning noble Goth), who, under Alaric, sacked and conquered Western Rome in 409–410 AD.[54]

The Pope also entered into the power vacuum, just as the conquering barbarians, but to restore civil order. Pope Leo I demonstrated the exercise of papal power beyond the walls of the Church on several significant occasions. In 452 AD, Leo I or Leo the Great, openly demonstrated the apparent authority of papal power to deal with secular matters when he met with Attila the Hun to persuade him not to destroy Rome. He negotiated with Attila on behalf of the City of Rome and arranged the tribute that purchased his withdrawal. Perhaps the Pope's fall-back protector should have been the Roman Emperor of the East.[55]

Pope Leo I even went to Constantinople at the request of St. Flavian, the then patriarch of Constantinople, to thwart the heretical Doctrine of Monophysite. This doctrine had all but displaced Christianity in Constantinople asserting that Christ had only "one devine nature" and that of God. Pope Leo also sought the collaborative influence and support of Western Emperor Valentinian III to defeat the heresy of Monophysite in the East.[56] In another instance

Pope Leo met the Vandal King named Genseric and persuaded him not to sack and plunder Rome.[57]

Pope Agapetus also demonstrated the use of papal power beyond the Church walls when he went to Constantinople to (1) appeal to Emperor Justinian not to invade Italy and (2) defeat the Monophysites' design on the Church of Constantinople.[58] While Pope Agapetus was successful in defeating the Monophysites of Constantinople, he found that Empress Theodora, Justinian's wife, was the main instigator of this heretical doctrine.[59] An actress and comedian, Theodora had Anthimus appointed patriarch without canonical authority in order to continue the propagation of Monophysitism. Pope Agapetus eventually had Anthimus removed from his unlawfully appointed position as Patriarch of Constantinople.

DEMISE OF THE ROMAN EMPIRE

Neither persuasive papal power of the west nor military power of eastern Rome were sufficient to thwart those conquering barbarian tribes known as the Vandals under King Gaiseric in 456 AD; the Heruli under Odoacer who defeated Romulus Augustus (the last Western Roman Emperor) in 476 AD and declared himself Rex Italiae, King of Italy, and officially ended the Roman Empire; and the Ostrogoths (tribal cousins of the Visigoths meaning splendid Goth) who defeated Odoacer in 493 AD under Theodoric the Great at the Battle of Ravenna and took over as King of Italy.[60]

These conquering barbarians were more than just military threats. They were purportedly practicing Christians, but with a variance. They believed in the Arian Doctrine

(Jesus was created, not born) and did not recognize the Bishop of Rome as head of the Church. Thus, they were not trusted by the Bishop of Rome and were considered an ecclesiastical and military threat to the Church.

The last of the true Roman Emperors was Justinian, a Christian who believed he was king and priest, and that it was his divine destiny to re-conquer and restore the Roman Empire up to its ancient borders.[61] At the request of the Bishop of the Western Empire, the conquering barbarians were deposed by Justinian. Powers of the papacy were restored at the conclusion of the Gothic Wars in 553 AD when Justinian, the Emperor of now "United Rome", decreed as Constantine that the bishop was vested with civil, political and religious powers.[62]

PEDIGREE OF THE BISHOP OF ROME

There were those who maintained that the Orthodox Church of Rome was founded at Rome by both Peter and Paul, and it was they who established and chose the first line of succession of bishops.[63] This undocumented claim asserted the apostolic pedigree of early bishops of Rome. Contrarily, Roman Catholics say that Peter founded the Orthodox Church of Rome. While there is much controversy as to who established the Church of Rome, there is no proof that it was founded by Peter or Paul.

Today, only the Bishop of Rome uses the title of Pope, who, according to Papal Rule, is possessed with supreme legislative, executive, and judicial authority in the Roman Catholic Church and is Head of State of the Vatican. As such, Roman Catholic believers are forbidden from using the title of Pope otherwise. This restriction, however, dates back to Pope Gregory VI in 1073.

THE EMPEROR AND RELIGIONS OF ROME

During the reign of the Roman Emperor, the State's pagan religion and worship centered on Roman gods. Worship eventually evolved into a practice that centers only on the Emperor as a god on earth. The title of the high priest of Roman religion was Pontifex Maximus, the highest and most important position in polytheistic Ancient Roman Religion.[64] The Pontifex Maximus was first a patrician in social status, who headed the college of pontiffs that elected the Pope. He was also in charge of and regulated all religious affairs and ceremonies.

In 381 AD, Roman Emperor Gratian, who reigned from 367–383 AD, was the first among emperors to reject the title of pontifex.[65] This was because the emperor was head of the Roman state religion, and responsible for ensuring that pagan ceremonies were properly performed. The emperor was also responsible for pax deorum, maintaining peace with the gods. Gratian was a Christian and could not be leader of the state church holding the title of pontifex maximus.

Gratian refused to wear the pagan insignia or use the imperial title of Pontifex Maximus. He bestowed this title upon the then reigning Bishop of Rome, Damasus I, making it clear that Christianity was the official religion of the Empire.[66] Damasus I then asserted authority over all bishops and became known as the first true pope. As Emperor,

Gratian also ended state subsidies to all pagan religions and cults.

Emperor Theodosius, a Christian who reigned in the East, had been relatively tolerant towards pagans. But he eventually banned all practices of pagan religions and destroyed their temples.[67] He too rejected the title of pontifex maximus, because the Bishop of Rome had officially assumed the use of the title. He sought to confer the title of Pontifex Maximus of the Eastern Empire upon St. Gregory of Nazianzus, Bishop of Constantinople, but he too rejected it.

THE ROMAN CATHOLIC CHURCH THINKING TO CHANGE TIME AND LAWS

After Constantine declared Christianity a state approved religion, the papacy started to freely wield political power in the West to further its existence, and used codified law to enforce its doctrines. Even though these doctrines were heretical and interpreted differently by the Orthodox Catholic Church, Constantine tolerated and supported this move because of his desire for social and political unity.

Constantine's tolerance paved the way for the introduction of heretical doctrines and paganism into the Orthodox Catholic Church via what had become known as the Roman Catholic Church. He saw the creation of the Roman Catholic Church as an opportunity to establish unity and peace in the State between Christians and pagans by fusing attributes of pagan practices as to doctrine, ceremonies, and superstition with the faith and worship of orthodox Christianity.[68]

The Papacy promoted Christianity among pagans and heathens by incorporating the use of images and relics into Christian worship, and mixing pagan practices with biblical themes.[69] This was possible because the second commandment forbidding image worship was eliminated by the papacy, and the tenth commandment was divided.[70] The fourth commandment was altered to set aside the Sabbath and replaced with the festival observed by heathens as the venerable day of the sun, *venerabili die Solis*. Sun worship is believed to be the earliest form of idolatry and the oldest component of the Roman religion.[71]

The pagan religions of Rome revered the Invincible Sun, Sol Invictus, as the supreme divinity in the Empire.[72] Constantine and his family were believed to be sun worshipers at the time of his conversion to Christianity. He desired harmonious relations among the sun worshiping pagans and Christian, and to institutionalize Christian significance into pagan festivals.[73] Thus, Constantine issued the Edict of 321 A.D decreeing that Sunday was to be observed as a day of public festival and rest throughout the Roman Empire.[74]

Constantine's Edict of 321 facilitated a pagan-Christian theocracy and state policy that viewed all citizens of Roman as Christians.[75] This perspective allowed him to view government as divine in its existence and mission, wherein church and state functioned as separate branches of government. This approach provided the means by which he could resolve social and political unrest among Christians and pagans whom he inherited as Emperor.

During the time of Edict 321, Pope Sylvester ordered the clergy to stop calling the days of the week after the names of their gods, e.g. the day of the Sun, Moon, Mars,

Mercury, Jupiter, Venus, and Saturn.[76] Yet, to refer to them as the first, second, third, fourth, fifth, and sixth day (feria) of the week. His justification was that in the beginning of Genesis, it is written that God said concerning each day: on the first, Let there be light; on the second, Let there be a firmament; on the third, Let the earth bring forth living plants, etc. (Gen 1:3 et seq.).

Pope Sylvester then ordered the clergy to call the first day of the week the Lord's Day, the day that Christ our Lord arose from the dead. He also ordered the clergy to transfer the designation of Sabboth Day from Saturday to Sunday as the first day so that all people could rest from work on this day.[77] Hence, the Lord's Day and the Sabboth were to be observed concomitantly.

The Lord's holy day (Greek for *kyriake hagia hemera*), a term that appeared around the latter half of the first century, is observed by most Christians in commemoration of the resurrection of Jesus Christ (Acts 20:7; 1 Cor 16:2). The true Sabbath was pronounced a relic of Judaism and the observers were declared to be accursed, which made the observance of Sunday as the Sabbath an act reflective of the Mystery of Lawlessness.[78]

In changing the Commandments of God's law, the papacy did indeed think to change the law and exalt itself above all that is called God, or that which is worshipped. One can easily conclude that the papacy of the Roman Catholic Church defied God's will for His original Orthodox Church of Pentecost, while concomitantly fulfilling the prophesy of Daniel 7:25, that is: "wear out the saints of the most high, and think to change time and laws."

The Western Roman Empire deteriorated greatly in legal, political, and military strength during the 5th and 6th Centuries. This was the result of military defeats by barbarian tribes that invaded Western Rome and other territories of the Empire. Powers of the papacy were also greatly diminished. However, the Byzantine Empire retained control over the West, and the popes of this era continued their dependency on the Byzantine Empire for protection and provision.

During the seventh century, the Byzantine Empire lost a great deal of its territory and political power due to the expansion and occupation of the Muslims. The papacy became resistive to the Empire's interference in papal affairs. As a result, Eastern Emperors retaliated by increasing taxes and prohibiting worship of all religious statutes and painting. The Roman Catholic Church, however, ignored these prohibitions.

The eventual decline of the Byzantine Empire and its effectiveness as protector of Western Rome and the Roman Catholic Church led the pope to assume even a greater role in Roman governance. Matters of defense, diplomatic relationships with foreign nation states, and finding alternative sources of supply were but a few of the extra-religious matters handled by the pope.[79]

Justinian's power and protection of Western Rome waned and the then Pope Leo III sought protection from the Carolingian Dynasty, the Franks or progenitors of modern day France, against the Lombards of Northern Italy under King Desiderius.[80] For this protection, Pope Leo III crowned Charles I, King of France (or Charles the Great, Charlemagne, son of Pepin III or Pepin the Short) on

Christmas Day,[81] as Emperor and Augustus. Papal ties with Eastern Rome were severed by this act.[82]

Charlemagne restored papal power in Western Italy and became guardian of Western Rome and the papacy. During his reign from 768 to 814 AD, he was eventually recognized by the Byzantine Empire as co-emperor in the West. The Franks divided the Lombard territory with the Pope of Rome, creating the Papal State of Rome that became known as the Vatican.[83] This brought into being a new Western Empire, the Holy Roman Empire. The pope was now king of the Holy Roman Empire, Bishop of the City of Rome, and Pope of the Roman Catholic Church.

The powerful Charlemagne Empire was weakened over time by competition for the papal throne and wars against Rome.[84] Among those events that weakened the papacy and Empire was the saga between Pope John XII and Otto I, King of Germany.[85] Pope John XII, son of Alberic II and whose name was Octavius, was selected Pope at the age of eighteen.[86] He was the embodiment and unification of secular and spiritual authority in Rome. He was also known for his proclivity to engage war, dalliances, and demonstrated immoral behavior in and out of the church setting.

During the tenure of Pope John XII, the Lumbard King Berengarius and his son, Adalbert, occupied Rome, Italy and threatened to take over the Papal State.[87] Pope John sought the protection of Otto I, The Great, Duke of Saxony, King of Germany, who also discovered that King Berengarius held captive Adelaide, the daughter and widow of Kings of Italy whom Otto did eventually marry for political reasons.

Upon entering Rome, Otto took an oath recognizing John as Pope, agreeing to defend him and not to issue any decrees without his permission.[88] The Pope swore in return to keep the faith with Otto and not to make any alliance with Beregarius and Adalbert. Thereafter, Pope John XII crowned Otto the Great as Roman Emperor—the first German Reich—in 962, the same office Charlemagne held in 800 AD. For this reason, Otto was said to be the true successor of Charlemagne.[89]

After becoming Emperor, Otto I broke his oath to Pope John XII by issuing the Diploma Ottonianum decreeing that future popes be elected in canonical form, and consecrated only after they pledged allegiance to the emperor.[90] This established German dominance of the papacy and made Otto I head of the Christian Community. Otto went on to establish the Church-State Alliance, giving money, titles, and grants of land to bishops and abbots for their loyalty and royal services, and made bishops local rulers.[91]

While Otto continued the war against King Berengarius, the Pope sought to make amends with King Berengarius.[92] Otto killed the King in 961 and deposed the Pope because he led a revolt against the him, even though it failed. Pope John XII then died, the actual cause unknown. It was strongly rumored that he was murdered by a jealous husband whose wife had been discovered receiving the sexual affections of the Pope.

The Roman Empire became known as the universal Christian Regent for God on earth. Charlemagne and Otto the Great had received their emperorship through papal power of the Roman Catholic Church, which claimed to be the imperial and sole elector since the fourth century. It was also said that the Empire was God's protagonist on earth, established to fulfill God's purpose; to protect and preserve the Church.

It is clear that when the papacy conferred honor and primacy upon the Roman Catholic Church among all churches, and the Bishop of Rome was viewed as being first among equals and given the honorific title of president, the Church had empowered itself to engaged in matters of church and state with unfettered ecclesiastical and secular power. This included making kings and emperors.

5

Deception and Dialectics

THERE ARE perhaps many human imperfections that caused humanity to replicate the same negative behavior down through the ages, regressing to the same inevitable results of apostasy and failure. To be considered is man's inability to understand spiritually the origin of his iniquitous nature and how the innate flaw of human imperfection called sin influence and change human behavior.

Fundamentally, this includes what happened at the beginning of time, in heaven and in the Garden of Eden, and why Satan has such vitriolic hatred for God, Jesus Christ, the Holy Spirit and all of God's creation. Human imperfections also comprehend the lack of knowledge about biblical and secular history of the nature set forth in Chapter IV.

Other compelling exemplars are man's failure to perfect an intimate relationship with God; or hear and follow the voice of his Shepard (John 10:27); or perhaps he is not submitted to his pastor and does not embrace the rule of subjection (Heb 13:17) (Rom 13:1–2). Neither has man understood the world he lives in or the schemes of deception and dialectics he is subjected to daily by the enemy. These dispositions of man, whether resulting from conscious or unconscious conduct, makes humanity a prime target for Satan.

Notwithstanding, I would suggest that the confluence of many factors (sorrow, tragedy, misery, grief, religion, social, political, economics) have contributed to man's continued failure. I would also strongly suggest, however, that one primal reason is man's iniquitous birthright (depraved, perverted and sinful) (Ps 51:1–17). This is sin, *hamartia*,[1] missing the mark.

DISAGGREGATING DECEPTION

In the Second Epistle of Corinthians, Paul expressed concern about the saints being exposed to doctrinal errors (heretical doctrines) and the disruption of his work by legalistic teachers. In this context, he is addressing doctrinal errors and legalistic teachings that were focused on the mind and intellect of saints. More specifically, Paul stated in 2nd Cor 11:3: "But I fear, lest by any means, as the serpent beguiled Eve through his subtlety, so your mind should be corrupt from the simplicity that is in Christ." This simplicity in Christ, *haplotes* in the Greek, means singleness of purpose in devotion to Jesus Christ.[2]

Here Paul identifies the origin (place) of deception as the Garden of Eden where Adam and Eve became vulnerable to and were deceived by Satan.[3] The subject of deception is God's created beings, Adam and Eve; the mind or soulish realm is the venue where it takes place in God's created beings; and its purpose is to corrupt the mind from the singleness of purpose (simplicity) in devotion to Jesus Christ. This corruption is in fact sin, the end result of deception.

More specifically, according to Gen 3:1–6, deception focuses on the sensorial attributes of God's creations, e.g.

sight as to the fruit of the tree being pleasant to the eyes, and taste of the fruit of the tree being good for food. For consideration also is the intellect in that the fruit of the tree was desirable for gaining wisdom. There is also the sense of hearing as to the ability to hear the Shepard's voice (John 1–4:27) or hear the voice of Satan, a stranger.

THE PROCESS OF DIALECTICS

In addition to the vulnerability of the mind and sensorial susceptibility of saints to deception, there is another component to the process of deception that is clearly demonstrated in Gen 3: 1-6. This is dialectics, a major deployment tool of deception used by the enemy down through the ages, whether as a scheme, wile, artifice or ploy.[4]

Dialectics is definitionally a (mental) process engaged through cognitive abilities of the mind and verbal exchange. As such, dialectics is neurolinguistic in nature; yet, its success depends upon the susceptibility and/or the impressionability of ones mind, and weakness of faith in God. Hence, the mind is the battlefield where this neurolinguistic process is used to instigate deception and it is played out.

At play on the battlefield is an essential component of dialectics, the tongue. While this is a little member of the body, it is—in and of itself—wicked, a fire, evil, and can not be tamed (Jas 3:5–8). The function of the tongue is to convey dialectic thoughts of the enemy and intended victim. As such, the tongue is used to engage in the communication of thoughts and ideas spoken to corrupt the mind and beliefs of an intended victim, listener, who is susceptible and/or impressionable.

Dialectics is a form of logic or argumentation used in syllogistics. Syllogistics is a process of reasoning, moving from a major premise to a minor premise via deductive or inductive reasoning, then to a conclusion. This form of reasoning, also known as Aristotelian Logic, is also described in terms of a thesis (major premise), antithesis (minor premise), and synthesis (conclusion).[5]

Syllogisms are persuasive in nature, based on assumptions believed to be true and conclusions that are also believed to be true. There is a difference, however, between truth and validity in syllogisms: a syllogism can be true, but not valid. It can also be valid but not true.

One of the most widely used forms of dialectics is Hegelian Dialectics. George Wilhelm Fredrick Hegel introduced Hegelian Dialectics in the 1820s.[6] He obtained the concept from a Jesuit School dialectics expert and thereafter refined the concept to his satisfaction. Hegel contended that all things unfold in a continuing evolutionary process whereby (1) each idea or quality (thesis) inevitably (2) brings forth its own opposite (antithesis) and (3) opposites are integrated and overcome in a synthesis (harmonization of differences or a consensus of different views). Hegelian Dialectics is used on individuals and diverse groups as a process to dialogue and reach consensus.

In order to defeat the evil which is taking place around us, we must understand the dynamics of dialectics, its origin, and how it is used by Satan. In the main, the human mind and sensorial faculties of sight, sound, taste, and feeling are in effect composite neurolinguistic attributes through which the dialectic process is actualized.

Dialectics is outcome-based and is used in many forms to bring the church into harmonization and conformity with the world. It is used to create chaos from order with the intent of reshaping and establishing a new thought, or idea contrary to orthodox thought, or a new way of being. Hence, change is the only thing that is constant.

Where ever the opposites of order and chaos exist in the church, as well as individual or group dissatisfaction, dialectics is available for use by the enemy to attack the church. As the enemy's weapon of dialectics is exposed, we must remember that Jesus Christ did not seek conformity with this world; yet, he advised believers to be not conformed to this world.

CAUSES OF SATAN'S HATRED

Not knowing (realizing and understanding) why Satan has such vitriolic hatred for God, Jesus Christ and the Holy Spirit can be detrimental to one's spiritual and mortal existence. Paul recognized that the absence of such knowledge would be fatal to believers (2nd Cor 11:3). So, what happened in the beginning that caused Satan to develop such vitriolic hatred for God and Jesus Christ? What is it about these beginning activities that God's elect should know?

God's elect must first know and understand that God, Jesus Christ and the Holy Spirit pre-existed the beginning of time spoken of in Gen 1:1 and John 1:1. Their beginning was self-existent and before the beginning of the first of all things, including all of creation. In this context, God also instructs that . . . before me there was no God formed, neither shall there be after me (Isa 43:10).

Moreover, he informed that "Yea, before the day was I am he...." (Isa 43:13). Yet, as to the beginning of creation, it is the commencement of time, order, place and power of the Holy Trinity's supreme divinity. All things were made by the word, Jesus Christ, and without Him was not anything made that was made (John 4:6).

Jesus acknowledged to some 70 disciples that: . . . I beheld Satan as lightning fall from heaven (Luke 10:18). Thus, when God cast Lucifer out of heaven, Jesus was there occupying His first estate held in heaven since the beginning of time as spoken of in Gen 1:1 and John 1:1. It was during this beginning that Jesus created the heaven and earth, Adam and Eve, and even Lucifer; a most perfect, yet iniquitous and profane creation.

It is plausible that Satan's hatred was generated by his eviction from heaven by God because of his rebellious conduct. For consideration also is Satan's defeat by Jesus after his post-wilderness experience, and there is his beguiling and deceptive conduct in the Garden of Eden for which God cursed him as follows (Gen 3:14 and 15):

1. above all cattle and beast of the field confining him to his belly and to eat dust all the days of his life;

2. enmity between Satan and the woman, and between his seeds and her seeds; and

3. the seed of the woman shall bruise Satan's head and Satan shall bruise her seed's heal.

These verses are no less than a published judgment upon Satan. They make clear that man will always be suspicious and fearful of snakes and will use excessive force to exact a fatal result upon them. This is eternal judgment by

God which Satan can not change, from which it appears there is no forgiveness, appeal, or parole.

Another possible reason for Satan's hatred is his jealousy of Jesus Christ, who was anointed and destined by God to rule all nations with a rod of iron. Thus, Satan's claim to the earth was given to a new ruler, Jesus Christ, whose inheritance is the heathen and possession is the uttermost part of the earth (Ps 2:8).

This dispossession or dethronement flies hard in the face of Satan's ego, having been known as the ruler of the kingdom of the air, or Prince of the Power of the Air (Eph 2:2) and ruler of this world or Prince of this World (John 12:31, 14:30, and 16:11; and 1st John 5:19).

If there was any ambiguity in Satan's thinking about his dispossession, it was clarified by God's instruction to Jesus when He said: "Sit thou at my right hand, until I make thine enemies thy footstool" (Ps 110:1). God's recognition of Jesus Christ as having dominion and power to possess and rule the heathens and nations was further emphasized by God, who declared Jesus to be a priest:

> The Lord hath sworn, and will not repent, Thou art a priest for ever after the order of Melchizedek (Psalms 110:4) and (Heb. 7:11–21).

One can easily infer from this discourse that Satan's vitriolic hatred of God derives from varied reasons. There are, however, two primal reasons: being separated from God's very presence and being burdened with the threat of eternal death and destruction. Some might call it displaced aggression as to Satan's desire to destroy all of God's creation. Regardless, Satan is committed to effecting eternal destruction and damnation of all God's elect. Whether this is to be accomplished as an accuser, by means of deception or heretical doctrine(s), the objective remains the same.

The epic saga of Adam and Eve is illustrative of Satan's commitment to the destruction and damnation of God's elect. The import of this saga is that Satan beguiled Eve and deceived Adam and caused them to experience a fate no less horrific than his own: spiritual separation from God and mortal death. While Adam and Eve were not evicted from the North side of God's mountain in heaven, they were sent by God from the Garden of Eden into the earth.

There is another plausible reason for Satan's vitriolic hatred that relates to his ouster from heaven. It was stated in Ezek 28:17 that God would even cast Lucifer to the earth and lay him before kings to see. Indeed, God informs through Isaiah that all the dead kings in hell were stirred up and raised up to greet Lucifer's coming (Isa 14:9). According to Isaiah 14:12, these dead kings inquired of Lucifer himself by propounding the following questions:

> How art thou fallen from heaven, O Lucifer, son of the morning! How art thou cut down to the ground, which didst weaken the nations!

These questions were rhetorical in nature given that the dead kings responded themselves by answering with responses that exposed Lucifer's ungodly heart-of-heart intentions:

> For thou hast said in thine heart, I will ascend into heaven, I will exalt my throne above the stars of God: I will sit also upon the mount of the congregation, in the sides of the north. I will ascend above the heights of the clouds; I will be like the most High (13 and 14).

Scripture says that after Lucifer was greeted by these dead kings in hell, having now seen him for whom he was, they attacked his ego by stating sarcastically that those who look upon him will ask: . . . Is this the man that made the earth tremble, that did shake kingdoms . . . (Isa 14:16). To have these dead kings mock him was indeed a powerful source of Lucifer's hatred for God. After all, it was God who laid him before these kings and the world to see in his fallen state of grace: from beauty, power and perfection to a most profane and impotent creature.

According to Isaiah, Lucifer publicized unequivocally that he will be like the most High. This contemplates the dispossession of God's rule and reign over heaven and earth; the possession of comparable Godly powers; and knowledge of the mysteries of God. This unholy ambition to be like the most High God was flawed ab initio. Where would Lucifer get the power or knowledge of the mysteries of God to be like God, the most High?

The basic topic of discourse between Eve and Satan in the Garden of Eden pertained in part to the knowledge of God (the sacred secret things of God); what this knowledge was about; and what it would reveal if discovered and discerned. The knowledge they sought was and remains the exclusive property and ownership of God. It is otherwise forbidden knowledge and, therefore, a mystery.

Satan never had this knowledge for his personal use, or to impart to Eve. Else while, his desire to be like the most High God would have been realized, and he would still be in heaven. The fact that he did not possess this knowledge to give Eve necessitated the need for a dialectic ploy that would cause her to question the meaning of God's directives as to (1) which fruit could be eaten, (2) why this limitation was imposed on them, and (3) concomitantly generate the desire to possess God's knowledge.

Why is this knowledge and mystery so desperately sought after? Simply to posses God's knowledge (*daath and yada*), to be aware, to have understanding and recognition, to be sure, or be as powerful as God. Mystery connotes a secret or the idea of silence. The mystery of God himself, as to his wisdom and knowledge, which was once hidden from humanity but is now revealed, was ordained by him before the ages for the glory of his saints (1st Cor 2:7).

The mysteries or hidden things of God and his kingdom were kept secret from the beginning of the world (Rom 16:25). These mysteries have now been revealed to God's elect through the teachings of Jesus Christ (Rom 16:25), the prophets (Rom 16:26), by revelation (Eph 3:3), reading of His word (Eph 3:4), the Holy Spirit (Eph 6:19)(1st Cor 2:10), and by God directly (Col 1:27). The condition precedent to receiving God and the revelation of his mysteries and secret counsels was first articulated to the disciples as being that which was "given to them to know" (Mat 13:11; Mark 4:11; and Luke 8:10).

This demonstrates that God gives his powers and reveals his mysteries to whom he pleases. God's knowledge and mysteries are to remain hidden from those who do not believe. This is why Jesus spoke in parables, to insure that unbelievers did not receive his knowledge and mysteries. Only those who receive the Spirit of God are given to know the things of God. This excludes carnal minded humanity from receiving things of God for two primary reasons: (1) natural and carnal minded persons view things of God as foolishness, and (2) they lack spiritual discernment to understand them.

There are many mysteries that have been revealed for the saints of God to ponder. Among them are the mystery of salvation (Luke 1:77–78); fellowship (Eph 3:9); the gospel (Eph 6:19); Christ (Col 4:3); iniquity (2nd Thess 2:7); and faith (1st Tim 3:9).

DIALECTICS IN THE GARDEN OF EDEN

That a dialectic exchange took place in the Garden of Eden between Satan and Eve is undeniable. As stated in Genesis 3:1:

> . . . he said unto the woman, yea hath God said,
> Ye shall not eat of every tree of the garden?

Here Satan poses a question to Eve as to whether God said you (Eve and Adam) shall not eat of every tree of the garden. While Eve's response was correct ("We may eat of the fruit of the trees of garden: but God said I can not eat of the tree which is in the midst of the garden, neither shall I touch it, lest I die."), the questions solicits a response of doubt, which is cognitive of a God imposed limitation. This single question establishes a classic foundation for dialectics in the form of a negative and contrary idea; a prohibition and limitation of Eve's free will designed to generate individual dissatisfaction.

The thesis (major premise) here derives from God's initial instructions to Adam (and Eve) as to what fruit of the <u>trees</u> of the garden may be eaten: "But of the fruit of the tree which [is] in the midst of the garden, God hath said, Ye shall not eat of it, neither shall ye touch it, lest ye die." It also brings forth the opportunity for Satan to present an opposite idea (antithesis), a challenge if you will, as to what God intended by his instructions to Adam. This opposing idea, also antithesis or minor premise, was presented by Satan to Eve stating: "Ye shall not surely die: For God doth know that in the day ye eat thereof, then your eyes shall be opened, and ye shall be as gods, knowing good and evil.

Eliminating all other questions and issues regarding which fruit is edible and prohibited, Satan moves to effect a synthesis, consensus or harmonization of his and Eves opposing views. Successful dialectics requires that two opposing views be negated to facilitate a synthesis or consensus of the major and minor premises. Satan attempts to effect a synthesis of opposites was achieved by instructing Eve on several things:

1st—you shall not surely die if you eat fruit from the tree in the midst of the Garden of Edon;

2nd—God knows that the day you eat fruit from the tree that is in the midst of the Garden of Eden, your eyes shall be open; and

3rd—you shall be as gods, knowing the difference between good and evil, and blessing and calamity.

At the time of her encounter with Satan, Eve was innocent; highly impressionable, and susceptible to deception. Her innocence was consistent with her birthright in that she was born into a Dispensation of Innocence, and God was her creator and cover. She had known no evil in her life, neither the nature of subtleness or beguilement (deception), or the nature of Satan's vitriolic hatred of God. Moreover, Eve did not understand or know that Satan was her natural enemy. These conditions and circumstances made Eve ideally suitable for Satan's dialectical ploy.

Was Satan's dialectical ploy against Eve successful? According to Genesis 3:6 and 13, Eve did eat fruit from the tree that was in the midst of the Garden of Eden. The approach used by Satan in his dialectical ploy against Eve was neurolinguistic. As such, his appeal was through her senses and their verbal exchanges.

The first linguistic expression by Satan was a thought provoking, calculated question: ". . . yea hath God said, Ye shall not eat of every tree of the garden?" (Gen 3:1). This question was designed to cause Eve to perceive a limitation imposed by God and become rebellious; to reconsider and doubt the propriety of God's instructions as to what fruit could be eaten; and whether Satan's instructions were more appropriate and correct. Some of the questions Eve might have been provoked to ask herself were these?

> Will I die if I eat the forbidden fruit?
> Will my eyes be open, and will I become as gods, knowing the difference between good and evil, and blessing and calamity?
> Will I become independent of God's oversight and the limitations He imposed upon me?

The dialectical ploy was successful because Satan was able to shift Eve's attention away from all the trees in the Garden of Eden that she could eat of to the one that was forbidden. This was accomplished in part through her senses.

Having eaten the forbidden fruit, Eve obviously found Satan more believable than God. Eve saw that the tree had intrinsic and extrinsic value. Intrinsically, she perceived that the tree was good for food and was pleasant, good to look at (sight); and she ate it for food (taste and feeling). Eve perceived that the tree had extrinsic value because it could make one wise as well. Eve was also emboldened by her realizations in that she was even encouraged to share this forbidden fruit with her husband, Adam (Gen 3:6).

Unknown to Eve, her first bite of the forbidden fruit was the commencement of her spiritual and mortal death. Additionally, the dialectic exchange with Satan that negated all of God's instructions was the tipping point where Satan began to exploit, devour and ultimately destroy Eve and Adam. This was accomplished by the subtle and stealthy introduction of heretical doctrine spoken cunningly by Satan (via a serpent) in the form of false arguments and questions (antithesis) against God.

Eve's spiritual and mortal defeat by deception relates specifically to her willingness to engage in dialogue with the enemy. Her thoughts were conscious and her actions volitional. Consistently, she freely and voluntarily allowed Satan to interpose himself between herself and God, and erroneously define for her what was good and life giving.

It is more than realistic to believe that Eve was within the ambit of God's protection during her tete-a-tete with Satan. God, however, allowed her, as well as Adam, to exercise the prerogative of choice: to choose good or sin. This is a divine right given by God to all his creation as free moral agents.

JESUS DEFEATS SATAN'S DIALECTICS

From Satan's encounter with Eve in the Garden of Eden to his encounter with Jesus' post wilderness experience, he failed to develop a new or revised strategic plan to capture his intended prey. As with Eve, the dialectical ploy used against Jesus was designed to commence with a question that elicited doubt, then denial of the word and power of God, and ultimately defiance of the personage of God. While the dialectic ploy used against Eve was successful, it was swiftly defeated by Jesus. Unlike Eve, Jesus was neither susceptible, impressionable, nor weak in faith.

Following his water and spiritual baptism (Mat 3:16), the Holy Spirit led Jesus into the wilderness for the express purpose of being tempted, *prirazo* in the Greek, by the devil (Mat 4:1).[7] After fasting 40 days and 40 nights in the wilderness, Jesus became hungry (Mat 4:2). It was at this point that Satan thought Jesus to be spiritually, mentally and physically weak, thus susceptible to doubt and temptation. This was a most erroneous assumption because when Jesus came out of the wilderness, he was filled with the anointing and power of the Holy Spirit (See Luke 4:14, 18–19).

Satan posed three situations to Jesus with expectations of tempting him. These situations, two of which included questions that were propounded to Jesus, were as follow:

> If you are the Son of God, command that these stones be made bread (Mat 4:3).

Then the devil took Jesus to the holy city (Jerusalem) and set him on the pinnacle (gable) of the temple, and said to Jesus,

> If thou be the Son of God, cast thyself down: for it is written, He shall give his angles charge concerning thee: and in their hands they shall bear thee up, lest at any time thou dash thy foot against a stone (Mat 4:5–6). See also Ps 91:11–12.

Again the devil took Jesus up into an exceeding high mountain, and showed him all the kingdoms of the world, and the glory of them; and said to him,

> All these things will I give thee, if thou wilt fall down and worship me (Mat 4:8–9).

In the first ploy, Satan posed a question to Jesus designed to inspire a challenge and doubt in his relationship with God, to test his bodily or physical strength as to hunger, his soulish capacity as to desire, and his spiritual strength. This approach, as explicated above with Eve and Satan in the Garden of Eden, is classic dialectics. Jesus knew definitively who he was in God, for God had announced, published and proclaimed from heaven in unequivocal terms following his water and spiritual baptism: "This is my beloved son, in whom I am well pleased" (Mat 3:17).

Jesus elevated, honored and believed the word of God- This is my beloved son, in whom I am well pleased- over his own physical hunger. Thus, he had nothing to doubt or prove. There was no reason to command stones be made bread, even though he was hungry after a 40 day fast. Having chosen to remain humble to God by relying on God's word, it was easy for Jesus to answer Satan by saying "It is written, Man shall not live by bread alone, but on every word that proceedeth out of the mouth of God" (Mat 4:4). This statement was an immediate coup de grace to Satan's first dialectic ploy to temp Jesus.

The second ploy to tempt Jesus endeavored to elicit spiritual doubt from him even as God's Son, then denial of the word (scripture) and power of God. Satan introduces this ploy by presenting the same question to Jesus by saying "If thou be the Son of God." While Satan may not have been convinced, the response was the same. Reiterating, God had said "This is my beloved son, in whom I am well pleased" (Mat 3:17). Thus, it is settled: God said it and Jesus believed it.

Actually, the second ploy presented to Jesus by Satan purports to only test his belief in the word (scripture). Specifically, whether angles would catch him before hitting the ground, if He threw himself down from the pinnacle of the temple (Ps 91:11–12). The deceptive nature of this dialectic ploy in fact conceals its true intent; to test whether God will perform his word and keep his promise by saving Jesus as stated in Ps 91:11–12.

Had Jesus engaged this dialectic ploy, he would have abdicated his faith in God and God's word, abetting Satan in his efforts to test God. Having discerned the true intent of this dialectic ploy to test God, Jesus responded again by saying again . . . It is written, Thou shalt not tempt the Lord thy God: (Mat 4:7). This response effectively defeated Satan's ploy to test God.

In the final ploy, Satan takes Jesus up to an exceedingly high place, a mountain, and shows him all the kingdoms of the world and their glory. Satan then tells Jesus that he will give him all these things if He would bow down and worship him (Mat 4:8–9). The dialectic approach used by Satan in this ploy is patently neurolinguistic, making an appeal to Jesus through His humane senses; lust of the eye or greed.

Implicit in Satan's offer is his ownership of the kingdoms of the world. It is recognized, however, that Jesus did not challenge the propriety of Satan's offer, or his lawful right to give him what he purportedly owned and possessed as owner (Luke 4:6). Nevertheless, unlike the previous ploy designed to tempt Jesus, the temptation here exist in offering Jesus the kingdoms of the world for the consideration of bowing down and worshiping Satan.

The effect of Jesus bowing to and worshiping Satan would have been to establish Satan as his god. As such, Jesus' acceptance of this offer would effectively deny, abdicate and terminate His relationship with God, and volitionally violate the first commandment: "Thou shalt have no other gods before me" (Exod 20:3).

Jesus was cognizant of this written word prohibiting other gods. He knew too whom he was in God: God's beloved Son whom God exalted above all, even Satan. Thus, Satan was and remains subjected to Jesus in all things as his created being. This superior position accorded Jesus the right and power to respond to Satan most affirmatively: Get thee hence, Satan: for it is written, Thou shalt worship the Lord thy God, and him only shalt thou serve (Mat 4:10).

SUMMARY

The lessons learned from Jesus' wilderness experiences are numerous. The most obvious being he was tempted three times by Satan, and did overcome them all by refusing to yield (Heb 4:15). Satan made a most erroneous assumption about Jesus in his humanity, that is he was weak after 40 days in the wilderness. Satan failed to discern that when Jesus came out of the wilderness, he was filled with the anointing and power of the Holy Spirit (See Luke 4:14).

Jesus remained faithful to God throughout His ordeal with Satan, even though he suffered in his humanity during these temptations just as all humanity suffers (Heb 2:17–18). His wilderness experience demonstrates to all of humanity his level of compassion and understanding for those who are tempted and suffer. The entire wilderness experience reveals how temptations are to be overcome: by faith and the word of God.

Satan's strategy for successful temptation is to focus the ploy of deception on a believer's spirit, soul, and body. The strategy is typically begun in a subtle, stealthy manner and asserted gradually and imperceptibly by varying means. The means or major tool deployed to begin the ploy is generally neurolinguistic dialectics, a process engaged through the cognitive domain (mind and senses) and perfected by verbal exchange.

This tool of the enemy, neurolinguistic dialectic, is focused on the mind of a believer who is susceptible and/or impressionable, and weak in faith. It will also work on believers who are strong in faith and not so predisposed to ploys. This is why we must always be vigilant in prayer, exercise our faith in God, and be aware that the enemy is always seeking whom he may devour. In this regard, we must always be aware that the venue and battlefield for deception is the mind.

A typical result of temptation is that a believer is subjected to doubt. Doubt, which takes place in the soul, is one of the principle outcomes of neurolinguistic dialectics. Eve's doubt derived from Satan's question. . . . Yea hath God said . . . (Gen 3:1). As for Jesus, Satan's questions were design to elicit doubt by use of the word "if" (See Mat 4:1–9).

Doubt is purely a mental impression, negative in content, which manifests in the form of a question, unbelief, distrust, indecision, and doublemindedness. It may evolve from a believer's lack of faith in God and the power of God to perform his word by keeping his promises and oaths.

However, we know that by these two immutable things, God's promises and His oaths, it is impossible for God to lie (See Heb 6:17–19). It is on this premise that believers have a sure, unchanging hope upon which to anchor the soul, a better promise inclusive of eternal life and a better covenant because Jesus himself is surety.

6

The Veil of Moses and the Lack of Knowledge of God

INDIVIDUAL AND corporate knowledge, and understanding of neurolinguistic dialectic is critical to defeating (1) deception and apostasy of believers and non-believers, (2) human failure generally, and (3) the failure of the Christian Church. I consider that a most critical contributing cause of human failure is the "lack of knowledge of God." My exploration of man's continued dispensational failures throughout human history supports this belief as the principle cause of human failure.

This discourse of thought presupposes that the effect under review (dispensational failure) depends on a cause (lack of knowledge) in order that it (dispensational failure) might have happened. Without knowledge, there is nothing to understand, because understanding derives from knowledge of a cause, and every effect depends on a cause for its existence.

Knowledge spoken of here is not of a secular origin, but about God himself as to his holy nature, law, righteousness, and his wrath. Secular knowledge precedes the existence of one's faith in any god. Spiritual knowledge, however, derives first by faith in God, Jehovah Elohim, the self-existent one.

A lack of knowledge can range from absolute abject ignorance to willful rejection of God, either of which can fetter man's consciousness to secular knowledge. As an example, God sent Adam and Eve from the Garden of Eden because they rejected his knowledge and law by willfully eating of the tree of knowledge of good and evil.

The Prophet Hosea delineates the lack of knowledge as swearing, lying, killing, stealing, and adultery (4:1 and 2). This prophetic word was realized in the life and times of the early Nation of Israel, for their behavior proved them to be morally bankrupt and guilty of spiritual adultery. Their behavior also revealed an irreverence of God and his righteousness. A particular instance where the Nation of Israel demonstrated such behavior was at the foot of Mt. Sinai.

It was at Mt. Sinai that the Nation of Israel, God's chosen people, his peculiar treasure, prevailed upon Aaron, Moses' brother and Priest of the Nation to build them a god to go before them (a golden calf—graven image—to worship)(Exod 32:1). This was contrary to the will of God (Exod 20:4 and 5). The people feared that Moses had been gone too long and would not return from his 40 day visit with God at the top of Mt. Sinai. Moses did, however, return with the Ten Commandments, the law or the Decalogue written by the finger of God (Exod 32:16), but destroyed the law when he saw the golden calf (Exod 32:15 and 16). This was indicative of his people having returned to idol worship.

The Nation of Israel is God's chosen people. Their being chosen by God, however, had nothing to do with a special affinity over other people. God chose them because it was through them that Jesus Christ would be born and become

Messiah and Savior. Also, because of his love for them and his covenant with Abraham. Additionally, God promised to bless all people through this Nation (Gen 12:1–3).

This lack of knowledge, ignorance, iniquitous behavior, and irreverence of God and his righteousness was not just unique to the Nation of Israel. In Noah's Era, people demonstrated the same behavior. For these reasons, God flooded the earth and destroyed humanity (Gen 6:7). During Abraham's Era, Sodom and Gomorrah were inhabited by people with the same aberrant behavior. So much so that God's vengeance was kindled and he burned Sodom and Gomorrah to ashes (Gen 19:24 and 25).

Prior to Moses delivering the first set of engraved Ten Commandments to the Israelites at the foot of Mt. Sinai, the people had promised and covenanted with God saying, "All the words which the Lord hath said will we do" (Exod 19:8). They covenanted the same thing before Moses' second visit with God on Mt. Sinai (Exod 24:3–7). As Moses descended from Mt. Sinai with the Ten Commandments from God, his countenance was radiant (See Exod 34:28–35). He had been in the presence of God for 40 days, and God's Shekinah Glory was upon him.

Moses glowed so much that he had to put a veil over his face-a covering or a thing used to conceal-as he approached the people, unveiling only when he talked with them. The veil was removed because the people needed to hear what God was saying through Moses, rather than focusing on what he looked like. Nevertheless, the radiant glow dissipated in time and ultimately faded away. As long as the glow was there, the people honored Moses as God's representative, and they became irreverent when it faded.

As we consider the ignorance, iniquitous, and irreverent behavior of the children of Israel, Prophet Hosea made it clear that God had a controversy with them because, among other things, there was no truth, nor mercy, nor knowledge of God in the land (4:1)(See also Isaiah 5:13). Prophet Hosea went on to say in Chapter 4:6; "My people are destroyed for the lack of knowledge: because they rejected my knowledge, I will also reject thee, that these shall be no priest to me: seeing that they hast forgotten the law of thy God, I will also forget thy children."

Much to do has been made about the veil of Moses and the significance of there being no knowledge of God in the land. Looking to the New Testament for clarity, we find that there is a correlation between the veil and lack of knowledge of God. The veil of Moses shrouded the Israelites and gentiles with ignorance as to God's Plan of Salvation. Addressing the significance of Moses' veil, Paul said in 2nd Corinthians 3:13 through 16 that the veil prevented the children of Israel from seeing the end or terminal point of the Dispensation of Law, and that their minds were blinded from this pending reality.

Speaking to new believers who had walked as unbelieving gentiles in the past, Paul admonished them not to walk as gentiles had; in the futility of their mind, having their understanding darkened, being alienated from God through ignorance because of the blindness of their heart (Eph 4:18). Even today, the veil is said to remain over their hearts in the reading of the Old Testament, and that this will continue to exist until unbelieving Jews and gentiles accept Jesus Christ as Lord and Savior (Eph 4:17 and 18).

The Veil of Moses 71

As explained in Chapter V, the knowledge of God and Jesus as Lord and Savior is a mystery, and has been since the foundation of this world by divine decree of God himself (Eph 3:3–6) and (Rom 16:25). Yet, believers have acquired knowledge and learned of these mysteries through the revelations God gave to Paul, as well as other Apostles, Prophets, Evangelists, Jesus Christ himself, the Holy Spirit, Preachers and Teachers, and through the inerrant word of God.

This means that understanding the mystery of the veil and its relationship to the lack of knowledge of God among unbelieving Jews and gentiles was not discernable during the Old Testament Era. The reading of Moses, which means reading the Torah or Pentateuch according to 2nd Corinthians 3:15, could not be interpreted to reveal God's Plan of Salvation. This is because God did no reveal his Plan until the New Testament Era.

As we are now informed from ages past, the sacred secret things belong unto the Lord our God: but those things which are revealed belong unto us, that we may do all the words of this Law (Deut 29: 29). Even though it is given to us—the elect—to know and understand God, we have not fully comprehended God or the word of God. He is too comprehensive to be known fully! This too is a mystery. We can only know what He has revealed to us.

Understanding the significance of Hosea's expression "no knowledge of God in the land", and why Moses veiled himself can best be discerned from the New Testament. Paul and other men of God explained the limitations associated with blindness of the minds and darkened understanding, and the veil of Moses.

These mysteries were not fully revealed in the Old Testament, but were hidden as types and shadows of good things to come, figures or copies of things in heavens, and that which is true. The Dispensation of Law was a shadow of the good things to come; yet, was not the very image of these things . . . (Heb 10:1–13). The types and shadows of good things to come is Jesus Christ with a better covenant and a better promise to us-ward who believe.

Atonement for sin through "annual animal blood sacrifices" by the High Priest was a type and shadow of the coming of Jesus Christ as Lord and Savior, who, by his own blood, entered in once in the holy place having obtained eternal redemption for all of humanity (Heb 9:12). Animal blood sacrifices and the works of men existed under the Old Testament and Dispensation of Law, while spiritual relations with Jesus Christ by faith prevail under the New Testament Dispensation of Grace.

Paul viewed Moses' veil as a symbol or barrier of Jewish people's failure to recognize Jesus as the true Messiah and Savior. Their minds are said to remain closed even today when they read the Old Testament. It is as if a veil lies over their heart concealing the true meaning of the Old Testament. This veil can only be destroyed by the gospel and when a person accepts Jesus Christ as Lord and Savior.

The fact of no knowledge of God in the land equated to a lawless society; one that is morally bankrupt, irreverent, ignorant (unlearned about God and His righteousness because they rejected Him) and guilty of spiritual adultery. This lack of knowledge of God in the land is once again demonstrated by God's chosen people, the Israelites, as they journeyed from Mt. Sinai to the plains of Moab before crossing the Jordan River (Num 21:21–36).

One might say that they were still shrouded by Moses' veil because they had not come to understand God and his righteousness. Without requisite knowledge, their understanding was still darkened. They obviously remained alienated from God through ignorance, being blinded in their heart.

Having now received the 10 Commandments and a second covenant, the children of Israel owed God reverence and obedience. Yet, as they traveled toward the Promise Land, they mumbled and complained regarding the circumstances and conditions of their journey. They also murmured and complained about Moses and Aaron, saying they wished they had died in Egypt, and that God bought them there to die by the sword (Num 14:2 and 3).

Central to not having their way, the Israelites questioned "whether God was with them and whether they could trust him." These questions equated to no less than testing God. God had demonstrated himself repeatedly. He brought them out of slavery from Egypt; led them in the wilderness with a pillar of fire at night and a pillar of clouds during the day; he facilitated their crossing the Red Sea by standing the waters up on both side allowing the people to cross over on dry land; he gave them water to drink in the wilderness, once by miraculously purifying bitter water (Exod 15:22–27); and gave them manna and quail to eat.

Notwithstanding the numerous ways that God had demonstrated His love for the Israelites, they murmured and complained, speaking evil of him. Having heard their comments, God's anger was kindled. He lit a fire that burned and consumed the children of Israel from the uttermost parts (outer perimeters) of the camp, and did so until Moses prayed to God and the fire was quenched (Num 11:1–3). God then questioned Moses, asking how long will these Israelites provoke him and treat him with such contempt in spite of all the signs and wonders he had shown (Num 14:11).

While God forgave the people, he still punished them (See Num 14:20–23), because they had disobeyed him with a most irreverent behavior and tested him 10 times in the wilderness (:22).[1] God had resolved to allow their self-fulfilling prophesy of death in the wilderness to be realized; just as he had heard them say (1 Cor 10:5)(Num 14:28 and 29). Accordingly, they were not allowed to go into the Promise Land (:23), but wandered in the wilderness for 40 years until all of the people 20 years of age and older died off, except for Joshua and Caleb (Num 14:30, 38). God said, I the Lord said. . . . there they shall die (:35).

The 40 year period equated to one year for every day they searched the Promises Land (:34). God assigned the 40 year period for every day the spies searched out the Promise Land (:34). This was to insure that Children of Israel had sufficient time to know that God had now breached his promise(s) to them, having never done so before (:34 and :35).

Having examined the Israelites irreverent behavior toward God from slavery in Egypt to Mt. Sinai, through their wilderness travels to Canaan, it can be said that they did not know or understand God and his righteousness. They were still shrouded with the Veil of Moses. Thus, the two covenants they perfected with God, agreeing to do all he required and the law given them in the Ten Commandments were woefully insufficient as barriers or deterrents to their iniquitous and reprobate behavior. They did not understand that God's promises stood forever, and that his word was immutable, and never retuned void but prospered in the very thing where he sent it (Is 55:11).

Even if they had a zeal for God, they lacked knowledge of him which is a dangerous thing. Had they understood, they would not have tested God as they did, complaining, crying, mumbling, grumbling, and speaking against God and Moses. They remained blinded in their hearts and minds, having willfully rejected God, his word, and his will for their lives just as Adam and Eve had done in the Garden of Eden, the people of Noah's Era, and those of the Era of Sodom and Gomorra.

There is a strong parallel between the life of Adam and Eve and the Israelites, respectively created and chosen by God. God was always in the presence of Adam and Eve. He provided them requisite covering and protection as they lived from day-to-day, and gave them one-on-one knowledge and instructions to live by. During their existence in the Garden of Eden, they were untested and had no evil in them to separate them from God, nor any righteousness in them to be commended to God. Adam and Eve eventually rejected God and his word for the counsel of Satan, eating from the tree of knowledge of good and evil. This was man's first sin, which separated Adam and Eve from God.

After God discovered that Adam and Eve had sinned, he made them clothing (tunics) from animal skin (Gen 3:21). The clothing made by God was an expression of his true grace and mercy. This was the first known act of salvation via animal sacrifice, which took place during the

Dispensation of Consciousness and the beginning of Adam and Eve's spiritual and physical death. Recognizing that Adam and Eve had come to know good and evil, God "sent" them from the Garden of Eden (:23) into the world for the first time.

God was constantly in the presence of the Israelites, demonstrating signs and wonders. There was also his knowledge given in the law of the Ten Commandments and the two Covenants he made with them. Yet, their iniquitous and reprobate behavior continued, resulting in the testing of God ten times, which incited his wrath upon the Nation of Israel.

I consider the worst of God's expressions of wrath to have been: the plague he sent because of their complaints against God and Moses associated with the desire to eat flesh; he literally burned them at Taberah; and ultimately required that they die-off in the wilderness after 40 years of wondering, forbidding them to enter the Promise Land.

Additionally, the Israelites kept "looking back" desiring the things of Egypt, e.g. life style. Lot's wife, whose name is not in the bible but according to Jewish folk lore is Ildeth (or Edith), died "looking back" contrary to God's instructions. Desiring things of the past and unable to just let go, she turned into a pillow of salt (Gen.19:26). This happened as Lot and his family departed Sodom, just before it was burned. She did not embrace the fact that God had sent his angles to save her life.

Looking back, the Israelites resolved it was better to return to Egypt, believing that slavery was better than the life they were experiencing in the wilderness. While life may have been rough in the wilderness, they could not see that God as Lord and Sovereign was always there (*Shama*), protecting (*Nisi and Saboath*), providing (*Jireh*) and healing (*Rapha*). Forever he is the God of Israel (Elohey Israel) and our righteousness (*Tsidkenu*) and so much more.

According to the collection of Hebrew pseudepigrapha titled "The Forgotten Books of Adam and Eve", edited by Rutherford H. Pratt, Jr. in 1926, the First Book of Adam and Eve reveals that on many occasions Adam and Eve longed for and attempted to return to the Garden of Eden. Sitting in the Cave of Treasure, a place located on the western border of the Garden of Eden where God had commanded them to live, they "looked back" in memory recalling their previous life. They complained and murmured about their being sent out of the Garden of Eden and the new world they had to lived in.

Adam and Eve would leave the Cave of Treasure and walk near the Garden's gate only to stand and cry, murmuring and complaining about their eviction and desiring to return to their previous life. On one occasion they almost lost their lives having ventured too close to the Garden's gate where stood an angle on guard with a flaming sworn postured to kill them. Life in the new world even caused them to committed suicide, but God sent his Word to raise them up.

The collective mindset of the Israelites was centered on satisfying their carnal, fleshly desires, e.g. eating certain kind of food and having creature comforts. Nothing, however, deterred them from fear, greed or arrogance during their wilderness experience. Nor could they see they had been ransomed by God from slavery for his purposes and not their own. They could not discern that "death of the self" was the way of God's deliverance from fear, greed or arrogance. The veil was still there because they had not accepted God and the knowledge of God, or Jesus Christ as Lord and Savior. Thus, as Hosea prophesied, the people were destroyed—in the wilderness—for the lack of knowledge.

The expansion of computer and printing technology has caused unanticipated exponential growth and availability in the genre of religious literature and related printed matter. Churches, synagogues, television evangelist, and many other non-profit entities exist to make God and the knowledge of God known to all of humanity. Even so, it is contended that all people have not heard the word of God.

The lawlessness and culture of corruption that prevails to day reflects man's exercised power of choice to sin. The denial of truth, false teaching and preaching, apostasy, intolerance and the lack of compassion for humanity itself, wars and rumors of wars are but a few human imperfections that leads to human failure. In the midst of it all are the wiles and schemes of Satan, working to cause deception and the utter failure of mankind.

Since the Garden of Eden, Satan continues to campaign for the eternal destruction and damnation of humanity. This is because there is no difference in the behavior of man in the twenty-first century from that of Adam and Eve and the early Israelites. They all left the door open for Satan to come in and steal, kill, and destroy any person of human imperfections.

Conclusion

GOD CREATED man a perfect being; a free-moral agent seized of divine right with the power of choice. The power of choice, however, recognizes that man has coexisting attributes of perfection and imperfection. This means that there is always the innate, though dormant, propensity to do either good or sin. Nevertheless, the power of choice is the ultimate expression of liberty God desired for all his created beings; from Lucifer to Adam and Eve, and all his human creation thereafter.

It is man's exercise of the power of choice that presents the opportunity for Satan to advance his vitriolic attacks. Satan knows that man does not know his own heart or mind and that his basic nature is deceitful, desperately wicked and perverse, weak, frail, and feeble (See Jer 17:9). Hence, he has the propensity to sin, he will sin, he will also deceive others, and is susceptible to deception through lust of the eye, lust of the flesh and pride of life (1st John 2:16).

A major contributing factor to man's susceptibility to deception is his failure to have understood why Satan has such (1) vitriolic hatred for God and His creation and (2) an insatiable desire to destroy man. Neither has man understood that the mind is the battlefield for Satan's favorite ploys of neurolinguistics dialectics, and deception. Nor has he understood the negative consequence of sinful behavior on salvation.

The premise has been advanced herein that man's continued dispensational failures are related generally to his lack of understanding the word of God and/or biblical and secular history. This lack of understanding results from the lack of knowledge of the orthodox word or doctrine of God and reverential fear, from which derives true wisdom and understanding (Prov 9:10). In other words, man has not been taught comprehensively enough or continuously enough to have acquired requisite functional knowledge and understanding of God and Satan.

It has been made clear by the word of God that people were destroyed for the lack of knowledge (Hos 4:6) (Ish 5:13). This lack of knowledge equates to man's failure to learn about and give serious consideration to God's word and his works. Adam and Eve typifies this failure in that they were sent from their first estate, the Garden of Eden, because they rejected God and His instructions.

Even though Adam and Eve had no knowledge of good or evil, and had never been tested by temptation, they allowed Satan to interpose himself between them and God, and erroneously define what was intrinsically and extrinsically good, regenerative, self-sustaining and assuring. By doing so, they rejected the knowledge, protection and council of God, and God sent them from the Garden of Eden and commenced the process of their spiritual and mortal death.

The experience of Adam and Eve was distinguished from their "posterity to come" because their relationship with God was face-to-face, direct, and one-on-one, with no other person interposed. God was their covering, they walked and talked with God, and he even clothed them when they announced their nakedness; a type and shadow of God's plan of salvation.

After Adam and Eve, God was faithful in sending his word and instructions to man (humanity) via His prophets and apostles. Even so, man was no different from Adam and Eve in that he also willfully rejected the word of God and knowledge to be gleaned from the word of God. Without the knowledge of God to guide him, man has been in search of smooth things (pleasant and acceptable words) and not sound doctrine from the pulpit. Men scratch their itching ears with post modernistic heretical doctrines as they embrace neo-orthodox doctrines of their preference, e.g. Replacement Theory, Cessation, Preterism, and Humanism.

It is contended by many Christians and critics of Christianity that people are rejecting God and his word, inclusive of the knowledge of God and the Church, because orthodox doctrine is not being taught from the pulpit, and the Bible is being taught selectively. This may be due to either (1) a failure of preachers and teachers to rightly divide God's word or (2) false preachers and teachers who willfully dispense false doctrine out of their own wisdom and revelation. In either case, it is gross error.

Failure to preach or teach the whole and uncompromised word of God, or to do so selectively, leaves a believer and non-believer without the requisite knowledge God intended them to have. God's word, even though untaught, is designed to save souls as well as to strengthen the faith and spiritual walk of a believer. If the word that is taught from the pulpit differs from the orthodox word of God, it is a fabricated, false and new doctrine that can only lead one to apostasy and eternal damnation.

Souls lost for reasons of a fabricated and false doctrine will be on the hands of the false preacher and teacher who is accursed by this lost (Gal 1:8). As a point of information, a preacher and teacher is synonymous with watchman, one whom God has entrusted His word and the souls of humanity. He is charged by God to "Cry aloud, spare not, lift up thy voice like a trumpet and shew my people their transgressions . . . (Ish 58:1). If the watchman fails to warn man of his sins as instructed by God or even impending danger to his spirit, soul and body, not only will that unsaved man die but his blood will be required by God at the watchman's hand (See Ezek 33:1–8). Preachers and teachers, as watchmen, must preach and teach the word of God as instructed by God.

The impetus for aberrant conduct from the pulpit may be attributed to the desire for fame and fortune as in Christian celebrity of today; to effect tolerance for religious diversity, including the so-called Christian hip-hop genre, to induce exponential growth; the syncretism or blending of religious doctrines to satisfy the post-modernistic needs of people to be accepted and validated by their own beliefs and associations because they have historically been rejected by organized religion; or the preaching of the prosperity doctrine that attracts and proselytes large groups from churches that do teach sound orthodox doctrine.

These are but a few instances where the powerful and confusing line of distinction between a spiritual (holy) lifestyle and secular ways of being is blurred. It seems that preachers in the pulpit, who in many instances are viewed as hirelings and entertainers, are at fault for inducing deception and apostasy in the body of Christ. They have willfully allowed themselves and the Church of God to be invaded by Satan by not preaching and or teaching the true word of God, or being watchful as instructed by God:

> How then shall they call on him in whom they have not believed? and how shall they believe in him of whom they have not heard? and how shall they hear without a preacher? (Rom 10:14). And how shall they preach, except they be sent?"(Rom 10:15).

This perspective presents an impressive foundation for continued deception, apostasy and the failure of the Christian Church in the twenty-first century. Our existence has mutated in to one that is corrupt and pathologically diseased, which tends to strongly suggest affirmative responses to the questions: "whether we have arrived at that point in time where it can be said "As it was in the days of Noah . . . (Matt 24:36–39; Luke 17:26–27), and "whether we have truly stepped into the Loadicean Era as a church (Rev 3:14–22).

False preachers and teachers are abounding in deceptive practices that subtly and stealthily introduce and perpetuate heretical doctrines that deny God and the knowledge of God. For this reason, we must reinstitute preaching and teaching of the true orthodox gospel -the good news- from the pulpit. We must also cry aloud and expose the practices of false preachers/ teachers/ hirelings who encourage false doctrine and apostasy.

This proactive approach includes exposing Satan's attack on the mind of the believer and non-believer as the battlefield where neurolingusitic dialectics is played out to destroy God's creation, man. No matter how simplistic or complex in design, the enemy's ploys of deception involves a skill-set that has been perfected down through the ages and should not be taken lightly.

It is surmised that human failure in the twenty-first century can not be attributed exclusively to the lack of knowledge of God in the land. There is also the case of impenitent ignorance and the willful rejection of God and the knowledge of God. This impenitence and rejection of God by Israelites and gentile non-believers shows that Moses' veil still blinds man's heart and his understanding remains darkened.

To day, humanity freely asserts a mindset of instant gratification and entitlement, murmuring, and complaining to get more or when expectations are not satisfied. We must not forget that man's highest end is to glorify God and enjoy him for an eternity. We must, however, die daily as to needs, desires, and expectations of our flesh. This requires being yielded and submitted to the will of God, and returning to the Assembly of the Church.

Murmuring and complaining is dispositive of a lack of faith in God to know our circumstances and conditions, and to perform his word. Such dispositions are sufficient to provoke God to anger and inspire his wrath, believing that man's murmuring and complaints equates to testing him as did the Nation of Israel. If we do not change our irreverent ways, we can expect the prophetic word of Hosea to become reality:

> My people are destroyed for lack of knowledge:
> because thou hast rejected knowledge,
> I will also reject thee, that thou shalt be no priest to me:
> seeing thou hast forgotten the law of thy God,
> I will also forget thy children (Hos a 4:6)

Endnotes

INTRODUCTION

1. C. I. Scofield. *Rightly Dividing the Word of Truth*. Online http://www.rapture.com/resource/scofield/scofield.html (2006). Dispensation in the Greek, oikonomia, means stewardship, management, administration or arrangement. The English translation of oikonomia means economy, the law of the house and/or a system by which affairs are conducted. In theological terms, the word dispensation refers to an era of time, of which there are seven (7) dispensations: Innocence, Creation, Conscience, Human Government, Promise, Law, and Grace. Some believe that the Millennium itself is a dispensation, the one thousand year reign of Christ on earth which ends with the Great White Throne Judgment followed by the New Heaven separation and damnation and secure eternal life. A dispensation consists of five (5) elements: a test for man; Man's failure; God's judgment; a rule of life; and a crucial event or crisis.

2. James Strong (1990). *Strong's Exhaustive Concordance of the Bible*, Thomas Nelson (1990). In the Greek, *harmartia* #266, derived in part from #264, means to miss the mark, sin, offense.

3. The means used could be by sifting you as wheat (Luke 22:31); to come upon you as a thief to steal, and to kill, and to destroy (John 10:10); and/or act as your adversary, the devil, as a roaring lion, walking about, seeking whom he may devour (1st Pet 5:8), or accusing the brethren.

4. Strong. In the Greek, false prophet is *pseudoprophetes* #5578, false teacher is *pseudidaskalos* #5572, and false brother is *pseudadelphos* #5569.

5. Jamieson et al. *Bible Commentary Critical and Explanatory on the Whole Bible* (1871) exegeting 2nd Cor 11:3. On- Line.http://www.jfb.biblecommenter.com/genesis/2.htm (2007). The aim of simplicity, as expressed in 2nd Cor 11:3, is to love Jesus with a singleness of purpose and affection. The enemy of simplicity is "subtlety" which is focused

on Jesus. This subtlety is functionally possible where there is fear.

CHAPTER 1

1. The Herald of Christ's Kingdon, *God's Sacred Secret and Its Fellowship* VOL. LXVI. March/April 1983 No. 2. Online http://www.heraldmag.org/archives/1983_ 2.htm (2007). The Sacred Secret or mystery of God is "Christ," the very embodiment, and the fulfillment of God's pre-determined Purpose of the Ages. He is both the expression of and the executor of God's Purpose! To understand Christ is to understand God's Sacred Secret.

The Herald of Christ's Kingdom, *The Pillar and Foundation of Truth*. VOL. LXVI. March/April 1983 No. 2. Online http://www.heraldmag.org/archives/1983_ 2.htm#_ Toc36864696 (2007). This writing discusses further the Mysteries of God. In Genesis 3, the Seed of the Woman and the seed of the serpent were foretold; and were shown as antagonists until the final crushing of the head of the serpent. Paul refers to these opposing "seeds" or organizations as the Mystery of Godliness and the Mystery of Iniquity. In 1 Tim. 3:15, 16 he writes that Christ personifies God's Purpose of the Ages; or as he calls it, the Mystery of Godliness. He indicates Christ's work as a man, and then as the resurrected all powerful Spirit, is in itself this Mystery of Godliness the Piety, the very foundation and pillar of the Truth. The Truth refers to the complete Gospel message as Paul taught it to the Church.

2. *Hebrew Language*. Online http://en.allexperts.com/q/Hebrew-Language-1605/ Image-tzelem-III.htm (2007). When God made man in his image, beTzellem Elohim, it was in God's spiritual and moral image, and not in a physical sense. Man was formed in the image of Elokim. This name represents the awareness that God is Master of all powers and He has total authority. Man in the image of Elokim means that man too, in a certain sense, is endowed with power and dominion as given by Elokim.

3. *The Image of God*. Online http://www.613.org/hasidism/09.htm (2007). This writing relates that the word image is translated tzelem, meaning a mold. Man (ha-Adam meaning all of human creation contemplated by Gen. 1:27) is the highlight of creation and deserves honor and respect for he carries the image of God. The word Tzelem

Elokim means the image of God. The expression "in the image of" recognizes man's ability as a free and intelligent creature, similar to God. However, the expression "in the likeness of" signifies man's course towards the attainment of this simulation, which can only be achieved through the collaboration of man and the Holy Spirit.

Jack H. Bloom. *Pursuing Tzelem Elohim, How I Ended Up Where I Started A Translator/Traitor's Perilous Voyage*. Online http://jackhbloom.com://Article/PursuingTzelemElohim.pdf (2008).

4. Ibid

5. James Strong. Sin is described in many ways. In the Hebrew it is called *chattaah*, meaning calamity, wretched, wicked, adversity; *avah* meaning or to crook or do amiss, bow down, pervert, do wrong; pasha or transgression, rebellion, revolt, or a state of lawlessness. In the Greek sin is *hamartia*, meaning to miss the mark, err, offend, trespass.

6. Ibid Perfect, *tamiym* in the Hebrew, means nothing need be added or taken away, spiritually mature, upright, whole, undefiled, flawless, or righteous; all imputed by God. Yet, perfection comprehends good and bad.

7. E. W. Bullinger (1960). *Figures of Speech Used In the Bible: Explained and Illustrated, 1898* and Companion Bible, Appendixes, Kregel Publications; Indexed edition (February 15, 1993)(2008). Figures of speech used In the Bible are most informative in there explication of Greek language usage in the New Testament, making known that the men who recorded it were Hebrew. Hence, the words of the New Testament are Greek and the thoughts and idioms are Hebrew, and the meaning of ancient writings was lost. The New Testament abounds with Hebraisms i.e., expressions conveying Hebrew usages and thoughts in Greek words. This most significant realization points out the ease of misinterpretation, the difficulty of doing literal interpretations, and the value of understanding Hebrew idioms in words and phrases. Thus, we must truly study to show ourselves approved unto God.

8. According to Gen 2:8, God planted a garden eastward in Eden, and put man there after he had formed him in the image of God. God put Adam there to tend and keep it (Gen 2:15).

A. R. Millard (January 1984). *The Etymology of Eden*. Vetus Testamentum 34(1):103–106. (2006). Online http://www.bibleorigins.net/BibliographyGenesisis

EdenEdinMaps.html (2008). Eden in the Hebrew is Gan ʽĒden, located near four rivers (Pishon, Gihon, Tigris, Euphrates), and three regions (Havilah, Assyria, and Cush which is often translated as Ethiopia). Most put the Garden somewhere in the Middle East near Mesopotamia.

9. To impute is to reckon or ascribe something to another. The imputation of Adam's sin was imputed to humanity because we are viewed as having acted in Adam as our progenitor (Rom 5:12; Gal 3:22). That is the whole person was in the ancestor and acting in him. God's remedy for imputed sin is imputed righteousness. First our sin was imputed to Christ on the cross (2 Cor 5:21; 1 Pet 2:24; Isaiah 53:6).

10. Generally, angles are created by God as mortal beings (Luke 20:36), full of power and wisdom (2nd Sam 14:17–20). They obey the will of God and function as ministering spirits to those who are heirs of salvation (Heb 1:14).

11. *The Great Division*. Online http://www.familychristian.com/chapter/14264.pdf (2007). Lucifer in the Hebrew language is Hillel BenShahar. The name Hillel came from the root word Hallel, which means, to praise, worship, adore. The implication is that Lucifer was the chief worship leader at the dawn of creation, endowed with gifts of leadership and creativity in music.

12. In *Ezek 28:13–15*, Lucifer is described as having the same characteristics as the future Bride of Christ as written in *Revelation 21*. From the description of Lucifer in heaven, we can see the following characteristics.

He was covered with precious stones,
He was made with tabrets,
He was upon the holy mountain of God,
He was made perfect.

The Bride of Christ is mentioned in the Bible as having the same characteristics:

She was made with precious stones (*Rev 21:9–10, 18–20*),
She was made with tabrets (*Jer 31:3–4*),
She was upon the holy mountain of God (*Heb 12:23, Rev 21:9–10*), and
She was made perfect (*Eph 5:25–27*).

13. Strong. The word deception gives rise to the words deceive (H-planao) meaning to roam from safety, truth, go astray, or seduce.

Delusion, a derivative of the word deception, means fraudulent, and straying from orthodoxy. Deceit in the Greek is dolos, meaning to decoy, trick, bait, wile, craft, guile, and subtlety. Iniquity in the Hebrew is *avah,* meaning to crook, do amiss, bow down.

14. Timothy S. Morton (1997). *The Difference Is In the Dispensations.* Morton Publishing (1997). Online http://www.biblebelievers.com/Dispen1a.htm (2007). The Dispensation of Innocence was established concomitantly with the Edenic Covenant (contract); the first Covenant between man and God based on God's promises. The Dispensation of Innocence is so named because Adam was created as an innocent creature with no natural propensity to do evil or righteousness. Adam did not become a sinner until he ate of the tree of knowledge, which separated him from God, ended the Dispensation of Innocence, and advanced the Dispensation of Consciousness. The provisions of the Edenic Covenant were as follows: (1) To fill the earth with the influence and order of mankind (Gen.1:28); (2) to subdue the earth to human uses Gen.1:28); (3) to have dominion over the animal creation Gen.1:28); (4) to care for the earth and eat herbs and fruits (Gen.1:29; 2:15); (5) to till and keep the garden; (6) and to abstain from eating of the tree of knowledge of good and evil under penalty of death (Gen 2:16–17).

15. *The King James Study Bible.* Thomas Nelson Publishers, Nashville,TN (2004). All references to Biblical Chapters and Verses through out this work were taken from the King James Study Bible.

CHAPTER 2

1. Strong. Sin is described in many ways. In the Hebrew it is called *chattaah*, meaning calamity, wretched, wicked, adversity; *avah* meaning or to crook or do amiss, bow down, pervert, do wrong; pasha or transgression, rebellion, revolt, or a state of lawlessness. In the Greek, sin is *hamartia* meaning to miss the mark, err, offend, trespass.

2. Ibid. The word perfection used in this writing is defined as *shalom,* which means complete, peace, perfect, nothing wanted or missing to achieve God given purpose.

3. G. Reckart. *Replacement Theology, Truth Or Antisemitism.* Online http:// jesus-messiah.com/prophecy/replacement.html (2007).

4. Robert Longman Jr. Online http://www.spirithome.com

/cessatio.html#cease (2008).

5. *What is the New World Order?* Online http://www.threeworldwars.com/new-world-order.htm (2007). *Gaia Worship, The New World Religion that Hates Chrtistianity* Online http://redeemedhippiesplace.wordpress.com/2009/09/15/gaia-worship-the-new-world-relgion-that-hates-christianity/(2009). Robert Gaylon Ross, Sr. *What is the Global Union?* Online http:// www. greatdreams.com/global-nwo.htm (2007). *A New Order of the Ages, Novus Ordo Seclorum. New World Order, Globalization*. On-Line http://www.theforbiddenknowledge.com/hardtruth/ newworldindex.htm (2007). *Preterism Defined, Defended*. Online http://www.preteristarchive.com/ PartialPreterism/pp_defined.html (2007).

6. Strong. The word deception gives rise to the words Deceive, which is *planao*#4105 in Greek meaning to roam from safety, truth, go astray, or seduce. A related word in the Greek is *plane* #4106 meaning fraudulent, straying from piety, delusion, error.

CHAPTER 4

1. Peter (petros) is not the rock or foundation stone of the OrthodoxChurch. Yet, Petra the true rock itself consist of Jesus Christ as the chief cornerstone, the original 12 apostles and their teachings and confessions that became the normative for the Church, and the prophets.

2. *The Birth of the Church At Pentecost*. Online http://www.vatican.va/holy_ father/john_paul_ii/audiences/alpha/data/aud19911002en.html (2008). Anne's Pentecost Page *Anne's Pentecost Page*. Online http://www.annieshomepage.com/pentecost.html (2008). *Passover to Pentecost*.Online http://bibleseek.blogspot.com/2006/06/passover-to-pentecost.html (2006). *Pentecost*. Wikipedia. Online: http://en.wikipedia.org/wiki/Pentecost (2008). Pentecost comes from the Greek word hemera for fifty, but the Jewish name is *Shavuo* meaning weeks or sevens.

3. J. H. Srawley (1900). *Early Christian Martyr*. Online. http://www.maryourmother net/Ignatius.html (2008). *Holy Apostles Antiochian Orthodox Church* (2008). Online http://www. holyapostlestyler.org/aboutorthodoxy.html (2008). A. Papadakis. *A History of the Orthodox Church*. Archdiocese of America. Online http://www.goarch.org/en/ourfaitharticles/article7053.asp(2004).

4. Papadakis

5. Ibid

6. Fortescue (1911). *Orthodox Church*. Transcribed by Geoffrey K. Mondello. The Catholic Encyclopedia, Volume XI. Published 1911. New York: Robert Appleton Company. Online http://mb- soft.com /believe/txc/orthodox.htm (2008).

7. *Followers of the way* (2007). Online http://covenantchapel .blogspot.com/ 2007/03/ followers-of-way.html (2007).

8. *St. Ignatius of Antioch: Early Christian Martyr. Early Christian Martyr.* Online http://www.maryourmother.net /Ignatius.html(2008). *Holy Apostles Antiochian Orthodox Church* (2008). *The Pentarchy* (2008). Online http://en.wikipedi.orgwiki/Pentarchy (2008).

9. *Holy Apostles Antiochian Orthodox Church* (2008).

10. *Timeline of Church History* (2008). Online http://orthodoxwiki. org/ Timeline_of_Church_History (2008). *Timeline of Church History*. Online.http://www.irazoo.com/ ViewSite. aspx?q=Church+ History +Timeline&Page=1&irp=1&Site=http://orthodoxwiki.org/Timeline _of_ Church_History (2008). *A Chronology of Early Byzantine World: Byzantine Cultures; East and West.* Athena Review Vol. 3, No 1 Online http://www.athenapub.com/9timelin.htm (2001).

11. D. Calhoun (2006). *Ancient and Medieval Church History: the Apologists.* Online http://www.covenantseminary.edu/worldwide/en /CH310/CH310_T_04.html2006 (2006). B. H. Swett. *State Church of the Roman Empire: A Summary Chronology.* Online, Swett, 7 May 1998. http://bswett.com/1998–5Church300.html (1998).

12. D. J. Love. *An Omission of Guilt.* Online http://www.sabbatarian .com/Content/ArianControversy.html (2003).

13. D. J. Love.

14. *Time Line of Church History.*

15. *Roman Gods and Pagan Rule.* Online http://www.allabouthistory .org.roman-gods.htm (2008).

16. *Roman Religion* (2008). Online http://www.unrv.com/ culture /roman-culture/roman-religion.php (2008).

17. *Early Christianity* (2008). Online http://en.wikipedia.org/wiki. Early Christianity (2008).

18. B. H. Swett. *The Beast of Revelation* (2000). Online http://www .pars.net/~lkwhite/ page/Beast/bst-ch3.html (2000).

19. M. Hunt (2005). *The Catholic Church and the Bible.* Online http: //www.agapebiblestudy.com/documents/The%20Catholic%20Catholic %20Church%20and%20thethe%20Bible.htm (2005).

20. *Holy Apostles Antiochian Orthodox Church* (2008). *History and Development of the Papacy Bishops in the Early Church* (2008). Online http://www.Religionfacts.com/Christianity/history/papacy.htm (2008). *Abridged History of Rome—Part II, Byzantine Rome.* Online http://www.romeartlover.it/Storia13.html (2008). *What is Orthodox Christianity?* Online http://www.holy apostlestyler.org/aboutortho

doxy.html (2008).

22. *What is Orthodox Christianity?* Swett.

23. *Timeline of Church History.* Swett. *History of the Roman Catholic Church-Part 11: the Church From Constantine to Gregory.* Online http://www.enjoyinggodministries.com/article/history-of-the-roman-catholic-church-part-ii/ (2008).

24. Hunt.

25. *Timeline of Church History*

26. Ibid.

27. Ibid.

28. Ibid

29. Swett.

30. *Timeline of Church History. A Chronology of Early Byzantine World: Byzantine Cultures;East and West.* Swett. Calhoun.

31. *A Chronology of Early Byzantine World: Byzantine Cultures;East and West.* A.E. Allen. *A Chronology of Early Byzantine World: Byzantine Cultures; Constantinople and the Basilica of Hagia.* Sophia Review Vol.3, No 1. University of British Columbia, Vancouver Online http://www.athenapub. com/9constan.htm (2002).

32. Papadakis.

33. Ibid

34. Ibid

35. *Eastern Othodoxy Eastern Othodox Church Oganization.* Online http://en. wikipedia.org/wiki/Eastern_Church_organization (2008).

36. Ibid. Fortescue.

37. *St. Irenaeus of Lyons: the First Great Theologian of the Church.* Online http://www. freerepublic.com/focus/f-religion/1808434/posts (2007). Jerusalem is the original foundation of orthodox Catholic Christendom and is the only Apostolic See that can claim this distinct honor.

38. Fortescue. Papadakis.

39. *Holy apostles antiochian orthodox church.*

40. Fortescue.

41. Papadakis.

42. Ibid. J. B. Calvert. *History of Central Europe.* Online http://mysite.du.edu/ etuttle/misc/Europe.htm (2005).

43. *The Western Church and the Culture of Rome.* Online http://www.stjohndc.org/Russian/orthhtrdx/e_P03.htm (2008).

44. Papadakis.

45. Fortescue.

46. *Petrine Doctrine.* Online http://en.wikipedia.org/wiki/Petrine_doctrine (2008). *Pope Siricius* (2008). Online http://en.wikipedia.org/wiki/Pope_Siricius (2008). Siricis (384-399) professed to be the legitimate successor of Apostle Peter, and the first Bishop of Rome to call himself Pontifex Maximus (supreme bridge or road builder between man and the gods) or Pope. Thereafter, Leo I (440-461AD), of an aristocratic background, was recognized as the first pope to receive the title of "the great." He was founder of Roman Privacy under the Doctrine of Petrine Supremacy, which recognized the Bishop of Rome as possessing universal jurisdictional leadership over all churches.

47. *Pope Saint Leo I.* Online http://en.wikipedia.org/wiki/Pope Leo I (2008).wiki/ Pope Leo I (2008). Leo I wrote copious letters and made some ninety-six speeches asserting the universal jurisdictional leadership of the Bishop of Rome over all churches. For this reasons, Leo I is acknowledged as having made great theological and doctrinal contributions to the Church, and, accordingly, was posthumously conferred the title of Doctor of the Church.

48. Ibid. Srawley. *Holy Apostles Antiochian Orthodox Church.* Papadakis.

49. Swett. *The Rise of the Papacy.* Online http://www.Hyperhistory.com/online_2/people_ n2/persons3_2n/papacy_rise.htm (2008).

50. Fortescue.

51. Swett.

52. *Decline of the Byzantine Empire: Collapse of the Western Roman Empire: $5^{th}-7^{th}$.* Online http://en.wikipedia.org/wiki/Decline of the Empire (2008).

53. Fortescue.

54. *Timeline of Church History. Chronology of Early Byzantine World: Byzantine Cultures; East and West.* Calvert.

55. Calvert.

56. Ibid *Monophysite Heresy*. Online http://www.neobyzantine.org/orthodoxy/history/monophysite.php (2005). The Monophysites believed that Jesus Christ had one nature, devine, contrary to the Holy Fourth Ecumenical Council of Chalcedon which asserted that Jesus Christ had two natures (divine and human) rather than one. The Monophysites of Armenia, Ethiopia, Egypt (Copts), South India and Syria have remained to this day separated from the One Orthodox Church of Christ.

57. Calvert

58. Ibid

59. Ibid

60. *Timeline of Church History. A Chronology of Early Byzantine World: Byzantine Cultures; East and West. The Beast of Revelation.* Online http://www. pars.net/~lkwhite/ page/Beast/bst-ch3.html(2000).

61. *Emperor of the Eastern Roman Empire, Justinian 1.* Online http://en. wikipedia.org. I (2008). Emperor Justinian viewed himself as priest and king, and supreme head on earth as to all ecclesiastical and secular matters.

62. *Byzantine Rome: the Rising Role of the Pope* . Online http://www.romeartlover. it/Storia13.html.

63. *The Pentarchy. St. Irenaeus of Lyon.*

64. *Pontifex Maximus: the Roman High Priest.* Online http:www.livius.org/pn-po/pontifex/maximus.html (2008). Apiryon.

65. *Pontifex Maximus: the Roman High Priest.* T. Apiryon. *Maximus.*

66. *Maximus*

67. Ibid

68. *Chapter 10: Historical Texts of Christians Meeting Together.* Online http://www.sabbaths.org/meeting.html (2008). The false Sabbath had to be exalted to an equality with that which was doctrinally true. E. G. White (1974). *The Mystery of Iniquity.* Chapter 45. Online http://www.preparingforeternity.com/fsr/sr 45.htm (2008). *How the Sabbath Was Changed to Sunday* (2008).

69. *Chapter 10: Historical Texts of Christians Meeting Together.* E. G. White. R. Bennett. *An Overview of the History of the Papacy.* Online http://www.bereanbeacon.org/articles/hist_overvw_papacy.htm (2008).

70. *Chapter 10: Historical Texts of Christians Meeting Together.* E. G. White.

71. Ibid.

72. Ibid.

73. *Historical Change of the Seventh Day Sabbath To Sunday.* Online http://www.theologyonline.com/forums/archive/index.php/t-12871.htm (2004). E. R. Gane. *How, When and Why Was the Sabbath Changed From Saturday To Sunday.* Online http://www.sabbathfellowship.org/biblestudies/ rwingane/biblestudy _gane_sabbathchng.htm (1997).

74. *Chapter 10: Historical Texts of Christians Meeting Together.* E. G. White.

75. *Historical Change of the Seventh Day Sabbath To Sunday.* E. R. Gane. During his reign, Constantine established the principal of

caesaro-papism, which placed the emperor at the head of church and its affairs. This principal was accepted by the Eastern Patriarch but rejected by the other Patriarchs, who refused to view the church as a secular institution and because the emperor did not have the spiritual authority to deal in matters of faith.

76. Pope Sylvester I (314–335 A.D.) *Decrees the Transfer of Sabbath Rest to Sunday.* Online http://biblelight.net/gift_of_rest_ rebuttal.htm (2008).

77. Pope Sylvester I. Note that the word Sunday does not appear in the Bible.

78. *Change of the Fourth commandment.* Online http://www.ben abraham.com/html/change_of_the_4th_commandment.html(2008). E. G. White.

79. *Byzantine Rome: the Rising Role of the Pope*.

80. R. Nosotro. *Charlemagne's Fight Against the Lombards and Saxons and Attila the Hun's Fight Against the Visigoths: A Comparative Essay.* Online.http://www. hyperhistory.net/apwh/essays/comp/cw09attila charleswars.htm (2007).

81. *Charlemagne*, New Advent. Online http://www.newadvent .org/cathen/ 03610c.htm (2007). *Charlemagne,* The Franks and their Kingdoms. Online http://www. robertsewell.ca/pdf/008Charlemagne.pdf (2007). *Timeline of Church History.* Pope Leo III crowned Charles I, King of France (or Charles the Great, Charlemagne, son of Pepin III or Pepin the Short) on Christmas Day as Emperor and Augustus.

82. Ibid.

83. Idid. Pepin the Short had conquered the Lombards before and given part of their land to the Pope. Now, however, the Lombards began to invade the Pope's land and threatened to attack Rome. Then Pope Hadrian II sought help from Charlemagne against the Lombards. Charlemagne restored the Pope's control. The Lombards like the Goths espoused the Arian Creed.

84. J. P. Kirsch (1910). *Pope John XII New Advent*. Transcribed by W. G. Kofron. The Catholic Encyclopedia, Vol.VIII. New York: Robert Appleton Company. Online http://www.newadvent.org /cathen/08426b.htm (2008). R. Chamberlin. *Pope John XII: The Bad Pope*s. Wikipedia. Sutton Publishing. (955–963). OnLine. http://en .wikipedia.org/wiki/Pope JohnXII (2003). M. D. Bawden. *The Deposition of Pope John XII.* Online http://www.vaticaninexile.com /TheologicalDiscussions/Papacy/JohnXII.html (2007).

85. *European Royalty: Italian Monarchies.* Online http://histclo.com /royal/ita/royal- ita/royal-it.htm (2004).

86. J. P. Kirsch.
87. Ibid
88. Ibid
89. Ibid
90. Ibid
91. Ibid
92. Ibid

CHAPTER 5

1. James Strong (1982). In the Greek, *harmartia* #266, derived in part from #264, means to miss the mark, sin, offense.

2. Ibid. In the Greek, *haplotes* #572 from #573 in the Greek means singleness, simplicity.

3. Ibid. Deception is a derivative of the word deceive, which is *planao #4105* in the Greek, meaning to cause to roam from safety, truth, or virtue; go astray, err, seduce, be out of the way.

4. *Hegel.*Onlinehttp://en.allexperts.com/q/Hebrew-Language-1605/Image-tzelem-III.htm (1999). Hegelian Dialectic, American Expose. Online http://www. Amerikanepose. com/hegel (2008). History of Dialectical Inquiry. Online http://www.valuebasemanagement.net/methods_dialectical_inquiry.html (2007). Raapana and Friedrich. What is the Hegelian Dialectic? Online http://www. crossroad.to/articles2/05/dialectic.htm. Dialogue and consensus-building (2005).

5. *Aristotelian Logic.* Stanford Encyclopedia of Philosophy. Online http://plato.stanford.edu/entries/aristotle-logic/ (2000). *Aristotelian Logic and Syllogism.* Online http://www. scribd.com/doc/ 13446672/Aristotelian-Logic-and-Syllogism (2007).

6. Hegel.

7. Strong. In the Greek, the word *ekpeirazo#1598* means to test thoroughly and the word *peirazo#3985* means to tempt.

CHAPTER 6

According to the King James Study Bible, the Israelites tested God ten times at the following places:

Exod 14:11–12 At the Red Sea, people complained fearing Egyptian Army would overtake them, and that God bought them to the wilderness to die; we told you while in Egypt to let us stay and serve the Egyptians;

Exod 15:23-25 People complained coming out of the Wilderness of Shur, they were without water for three days; the water at Marah was biter, and God threw Moses a tree which sweetened the water making it drinkable;

Exod 16:1-3 In the Wilderness of Sin, people complained about the journey

Num 11:6-9 and lack of food saying they wish they had died in Egypt, that God had bought them to the wilderness to kill them, and God gave them manna;

Exod 16: In the Wilderness of Sin, people gathered more manna than they needed, the next morning it was with worms and did stink;

Exod 16: In the Wilderness of Sin, people were told to gather more thanenough manna on the 6th day for the Sabbath as well, but some went to gather manna on the Sabbath and there was none;

Exod 17:2 At Rephidim coming out of the wilderness of sin, the people complained because there was no water, and Moses said they were tempting God, and they said God bought them there to kill them with thirst; Moses smote the rock as God instructed and the place was called Massah (a place of testing) and Mirabah because they tempted the Lord;

Exod 32 At Mt Sinai, the people bid Aaron to make them a gold calf for a god to worship, because Moses had been gone 40 days and feared dead;

Num 11:1-3 At Taberah, people complained about manna and God burned them from the ottermost area of the camp until Moses prayed to God, who quenched the fire;

Num 11:4-33 At Kibroth-Hattaavah, people lusted for flesh saying they had flesh in Egypt, and God sent them quail by strong wind of wind of the sea, and He sent a plague that killed the people as they ate;

Num 14 At Kadesh the people complained saying they wish they had died in Egypt or in the wilderness, that they did not want to go into the Promise Land because there were giants there.

Bibliography

Abrams, C. *The Mystery of God's Will*. Onlinehttp://www.bible-truth.org/myst-4.htm

Abridged History of Rome—Part II, Byzantine Rome. Online http://www.romeartlover.it/Storia13.html (2008).

A Chronology of Early Byzantine World: Byzantine Cultures; East and West. Athena Review Vol. 3, No 1 Online http://www.athenapub.com/9timelin.htm(2001).

Allen, A. E. *A Chronology of Early Byzantine World: Byzantine Cultures;*

———. *Constantinople and the Basilica of Hagia .Sophia Review* Vol.3, No 1. University of British Columbia, Vancouver Onlinehttp://www.athenapub.com/9constan.htm (2002).

A New Order of the Ages, Novus Ordo Seclorum, New World Order, Globalization. Online http://www.theforbiddenknowledge.com/hardtruth/ newworldindex.htm (2007).

Anne's Pentecost Page. Online http://www.annieshomepage.com/pentecost.html (2008).

Apiryon, T. *The Role and Function of Thelemic Clergy In Ecclesia Gnostica Catholica*. The Christian Apostolic Succession. Ordo Templi Orientis USA (1997).

Aristotelian Logic. Stanford Encyclopedia of Philosophy (2007). Online http://plato. stanford.edu/entries/aristotle-logic/ (2000).

Aristotelian Logic and Syllogism (2007). Online http://www.scribd.com/doc/ 13446672/Aristolelian-Logic-and-Syllogism

Bawden, M.D. *The Deposition of Pope John XII*. Online http://www.vaticaninexile.com/TheologicalDiscussions/Papacy/JohnXII.Html (2007).

Bennett, R. *An Overview of the History of the Papacy*. Online http://www.bereanbeacon.org/articles/hist_overvw_papacy.htm (2008).

Bloom, Jack , H. (2008). *Pursuing Tzelem Elohim, How I Ended Up Where I Started A Translator/Traitor's Perilous Voyage.* Online http://jackhbloom.comp://jackhbloom.com/Articles/Pursuing TzelemElohim.pdf

Bullinger, E. W. (1960). *Figures of Speech Used In the Bible: Explained and Illustrated, 1898* and Companion Bible, Appendixes, Kregel Publications; Indexed edition (February 15, 1993)

Byzantine Rome: the Rising Role of the Pope. Online http://www.romeartlover.it/Storia13.html

Calhoun, D. *Ancient and Medieval Church History: the Apologists.* Online http://www.covenantseminary.edu/worldwide/en/CH310/CH310_T_04.html2006 (2006).

Calvert, J.B. *History of Central Europe.* Online http://mysite.du.edu/etuttle/misceurope.htm (2005).

Chamberlin, R. *Pope John XII: The Bad Pope*s. Wikipedia. Sutton Publishing.955–963. Online http://en.wikipedia.org/wiki/Pope JohnXII (2008).

Change of the Fourth Commandment. Online http://www.benabraham.com/html/change_of_the_4th_commandment.html (2008).

Chapter 10: Historical Texts of Christians Meeting Together. Online http://www.sabbaths.org/meeting.html (2008).

Charlemagne, New Advent. Online http://www.newadvent.org/cathen/03610c.htm (2007).

Charlemagne, The Franks and their Kingdoms. Online http://www.robertsewell.ca/pdf/008Charlemagne.pdf (2007).

Decline of the Byzantine Empire: Collapse of the Western Roman Empire: 5th–7th Century. Online http://en.wikipedia.org/wiki/Decline of the Empire (2008).

Early Christianity. Online Available at: http://en.wikipedia.org/wiki/ Early Christianity (2008).

Eastern Orthodoxy Eastern Orthodox Church Organization. Online http://en.wikipedia.org/wiki/Eastern_Church_organization (2008).

Emperor of the Eastern Roman Empire, Justinian 1. Online http://en.wikipedia.org.wiki/Justinian I (2008).

European Royalty: Italian Monarchies. Online http://histclo.com/royal/ita/royal-ita/royal-it.htm (2004).

Followers of the Way. Online http://covenantchapel.blogspot.com/2007/03/followers-of-way.html (2007).

Fortescue, A. *Orthodox Church.* Transcribed by Geoffrey K. Mondello. The Catholic Encyclopedia, Volume XI. Published 1911. New York: Robert Appleton Company. Online http://mb- soft.com/believe/txc/orthodox.htm (2008).

Gaia Worship, The New World Religion that Hates Christianity. Online http://redeemedhippiesplace.wordpress.com/2009/09/15/gaia-worship-the-new-world-relgion-that-hates-christianity/ (2009).

Gane, E. R. *How, When and Why Was the Sabbath Changed From Saturday To Sunday.* Online http://www.sabbathfellowship.org/biblestudies/ erwingane/biblestudy_gane_sabbathchng.htm (1997).

Hebrew Language. http://en.allexperts.com/q/Hebrew-Language-1605/Image-tzelem-III.htm.

Hegel, G. W. F. *The Dialectic of History, 1812–1820*, From: George Wilhelm Friedrich Hegel, The Logic of Hegel, trans. William Wallace, (Oxford: Clarendon Press, 1874), Paul Halsall, January 1999. Online http://www.fordham.edu/halsall/mod/hegel-summary.html.

Hegelian Dialectic, American Expose. Online http://www. Amerikanepose.com/hegel (2008).

Historical Change of the Seventh Day Sabbath To Sunday. Online http://www.theologyOnlinecom/forums/archive/index.php/t-12871.htm (2004).

History of Charlemenge, Charles the Great, 768–814. History World. Online http://www.historyworld.net/wrldhis/ PlainTextHistories.asp?historyid= aa20 (2008).

History and Development of the Papacy Bishops In The Early Church. Online http://www. Religionfacts.com/Christianity/history/papacy.htm (2008).

History of Dialectical Inquiry. Online http://www.valuebasemanagement.net/methods_ dialectical_inquiry.html (2007).

History of St. Ignatius of Antioch. Online http://www.stignatiusecc.org/Ignatius.php (2008).

History of the Roman Catholic Church-Part 11: The Church From Constantine To Gregory. Onlinehttp://www.enjoyinggodministries.com/ article/history-of-the-roman-catholic-church-part-ii/ (2008).

Holy Apostles Antiochian Orthodox Church. Online http://www.holyapostlestyler.org/aboutorthodoxy.html (2008).

How the Sabbath Was Changed To Sunday. Online http://www.pathlights.com/ theselastdays/tracts/tract_22a.htm (2008).

Hunt, M. *The Catholic Church and the Bible.* Onlinehttp://www.agapebiblestudy.com/documents/The%20Catholic%20Catholic%20Church%20and%20the%20Bible.htm (2005).

Imperial Cult (Ancient Rome). Wikipeda. Online http://en.wikipedia.org/wiki/Imperialcult (2008).

Jamieson-Fausset-Brown. *Bible Commentary Critical and Explanatory on the Whole Bible* (1871) exegeting 2nd Cor 11:3. Online http://www.jfb.biblecommenter. com/genesis/2.htm (2007).

Kirsch, J.P. *Pope John XII New Advent.* Transcribed by W. G. Kofron. The Catholic Encyclopedia, Vol.VIII. New York: Robert Appleton Company. Online http://www.newadvent.org/cathen/08426b.htm (2008).

Longman, Robert. *Cessationism.* Online http://www.spirithome.com/cessatio.html#cease (2008).

Love, D. J. *An Amission of Guilt.* Online http://www. sabbatarian.com/Content/ArianControversy.html (2003).

Maximus. Online http://en.wikipedia.org/wiki/PontifexMaximus (2008).

Millard, A. R. (January 1984). *The Etymology of Eden.* Vetus Testamentum 34(1):103–6. (2006). http://www.bibleorigins.net/Bibliography Genesisis EdenEdinMaps.html (2008).

Monophysite Heresy. Online http://www.neobyzantine.org/orthodoxy/history/monophysite.php (2005)

Morton, T. S. *The Difference Is In the Dispensations.* Morton Publishing (1997). Online http://www.biblebelievers.com/Dispen1a.htm.

Nosotro, R. *Charlemagne's Fight Against the Lombards and Saxons and Attila the Hun's Fight Against the Visigoths: A Comparative Essay.* Onlinehttp://www.hyperhistory.net/apwh/essays/comp/cw09attilacharleswars.htm (2007).

Papadakis, A. *History of the Orthodox Church.* Archdiocese of America. Online http://www.goarch.org/en/ourfaitharticles/article7053.asp (2004).

Passover. Online http://onlinedictionary.datasegment.com/word/Pentecost (2008).

Passover to Pentecost . Online http://bibleseek.blogspot.com/2006/06/passover-to-pentecost.html (2006).

Pentecost. Wikipedia. Online: http://en.wikipedia.org/wiki/Pentecost (2008).

Petrine Doctrine. Online http://en.wikipedia.org/wiki/Petrine_doctrine (2008).

Pontifex Maximus: The Roman High Priest. Online http:www.livius.org/pn-po/pontifex/maximus.html (2008).

Pope Saint Leo I. Online http://en.wikipedia.org/wiki/Pope Leo I (2008) .wiki/Pope Leo I (2008).

Pope Siricius. http://en.wikipedia.org/wiki/Pope_Siricius (2008).

Pope Sylvester I (314–335 A.D.). Decrees the Transfer of Sabbath Rest To Sunday. Online http://biblelight.net/gift_of_rest_ rebuttal.htm (2008).

Preterism Defined, Defended. Online http://www.preteristarchive.com / PartialPreterism/pp_defined.html (2007).

Raapana, N. and Friedrich, N. *What is the Hegelian Dialectic?* Online http://www.crossroad.to/articles2/05/dialectic.htm. Dialogue and consensus-building (2005).

Reckart, G. *Replacement Theology, Truth Or Antisemitism*. Online http://jesus-messiah.com/prophecy/replacement.html (2007).

Roman Gods and Pagan Rule. Online http://www.allabouthistory.org.roman-gods.htm (2008).

Roman Religion. Online http://www.unrv.com/ culture/roman-culture/roman-religion.php_(2008).

Ross, R. G. *What is the Global Union?*(2007) Online http://www.greatdreams.com/global-nwo.htm

Scofield, C. I. *Rightly Dividing the Word of Truth*. Online http://www.rapture.com/scofield/scofield.html

Srawley, J. H. (1900). *Early Christian Writings. Additional Notes: The Epistles of St. Ignatius*. Society for Promoting Christian Knowledge. Online http://www.earlychristianwritings.com/srawley/index.html.

St. Ignatius of Antioch: Early Christian Martyr. Online http://www.maryourmother.net/Ignatius.html (2008).

Bibliography

St. Irenaeus of Lyons: the First Great Theologian of the Church. Onlinehttp://www.freerepublic.com/focus/f-religion/1808434/posts (2007).

Strong, J. *Strong's Exhaustive Concordance of the Bible*, Thomas Nelson (1990).

Swett, B. H. *State Church of the Roman Empire: A Summary Chronology.* Online Swett7 May 1998http://bswett.com/1998-5Church300.html (1998).

The Beast of Revelation. Online http://www.pars.net/~lkwhite/page/Beast/bst-ch3.html (2000).

The Birth of the Church At Pentecost. Online http://www.vatican.va/holy_father/john_paul_ii/audiences/alpha/data/aud19911002en.html (2008).

The Great Division. http://www.familychristian.com/chapters/14264.pdf (2007).

The Herald of Christ's Kingdon, *God's Sacred Secret and Its Fellowship* VOL. LXVI. March/April 1983 No. 2. http://www.heraldmag.org/archives/1983_2.htm.

The Herald of Christ's Kingdom, *The Pillar and Foundation of Truth.* VOL. LXVI. March/April 1983 No. 2. http://www.heraldmag.org/archives/1983_2.htm#_Toc36864696.

The Image of God. http://www.613.org/hasidism/09.htm.

The King James Study Bible. Thomas Nelson Publishers, Nashville, TN.

The New Advent. *Pope St. Leo I (The Great).* Online http://www.newadvent.org/cathen/09154b.htm (2007).

The Pentarchy. Onlinehttp://en.wikipedi.org/wiki/Pentarchy (2008).

The Rise of the Papacy. Online http://www.Hyperhistory.com/online_2/people_n2/persons3_2n/papacy_rise.htm (2008).

The Western Church and the Culture of Rome. On- Line. http://www.stjohndc.org/Russian/orthhtrdx/e_P03.htm (2008).

Timeline of Church History. Online http://orthodoxwiki.org/Timeline_of_Church_History (2008).

Timeline of Church History. Onlinehttp://www.irazoo.com/ViewSite.aspx?q=Church+History+Timeline&Page=1&irp=1&Site=http://orthodoxwiki.org/Timeline_of_Church_History

What is the New World Order?. Online http://www.threeworldwars.com/new-world-order.htm (2007).

What Is Orthodox Christianity? Online http://www.holyapostlestyler.org/aboutorthodoxy.html (2008).

White, G. E. (1974). *The Mystery of Iniquity*. Chapter 45. Online http://www.preparingforeternity.com/sr/sr45.htm

www.ingramcontent.com/pod-product-compliance
Lightning Source LLC
Chambersburg PA
CBHW070923160426
43193CB00011B/1561